I0773577

Restore the USA

Start a Non-Violent Revolution to Restore Limited Government Under the Constitution; Use 'Gold as Money' (prices by weight of 24ct), Private Mints, No Fed. This will bring more Liberty, Peace, Justice, Morality, and Prosperity to the USA.

Author: David Redick

Edition	Issue Date	Pages
First	August-2016	208
Current , 2d	August-2017	222

Published by 'Safer Investing Group (SaferInvesting.org)

Library of Congress: ISBN-13: 978-1537376516 ,
ISBN-10: 1537376519

Printed in the USA by CreateSpace.com, a DBA of On-Demand Publishing LLC, part of the Amazon group of companies.

This book is available at on-line services such as Amazon.com. Other books by Dave are there also. See the list at p. 218.

This book is dedicated to all citizens of the USA. I hope the information it offers will activate the thinking of many citizens, and that they will take action to correct the abuses by our government officials. This will lead to more Liberty, Peace, Prosperity and Justice.

Wise Thoughts ....

Some seekers of monetary reform want the abolition of central banking and a full separation of money from the state, through a monetary system based on competitive, private free banking. Prof. Richard Ebeling (Citadel.edu) commented on this statement; "This is the ultimate and most reasonable of all the alternatives to the existing system of monetary central planning through the government institution of central banks."

"The only thing necessary for the triumph of evil is for good people to do nothing.", Edmund Burke

"Resistance is not futile, but the most constructive and noble stance of all.", Lew Rockwell (Mises.org, Lew Rockwell.com)

"There are lots of bad governments in this world. The only bad government we have a right or obligation to change is the one in Washington, D.C.", Charley Reese

"Principles are intended especially to guide our behavior in difficult times. If they don't do so, then our proclaimed principles stand revealed as having been nothing but rhetoric.", Robert Higgs (Independent.org)

"A nation of sheep will beget a government of wolves.", Edward R. Murrow

"Those who control us are not going to give up their control without a world war. In the United States evil has seized power from the people, and evil will not give it back.", Dr. Paul Craig Roberts (PaulCraigRoberts.org)

An evil thought that Dave fights in this book: ""Give me control of a nation's money and I care not who makes its' laws" – 1790, Mayer Amschel Bauer Rothschild (1743 -1812), Founder of the worldwide Rothschild Banking Dynasty.

Table of Contents

****

Special Topics:

Introduction

Definition of Revolution: Activity or movement designed to cause fundamental changes in a socioeconomic situation. (Merriam-Webster)

****

This book is written to educate a broad audience, from citizens and students, to professors, politicians, generals, business leaders, and bankers, on what is wrong with the USA, and world, political, industrial, social, and monetary systems, and how to fix them. These systems have brought the USA, and most nations in the world, to the brink of economic and social collapse, which history shows that politicians often try to avoid by starting wars. This one could be a nuclear WW3!

The USA needs a Movement and Revolution (non-violent) to end distortions and losses in our economy and culture, and corruption in government and the financial services industry (more on p. 12).

Our Revolution is named 'Forward USA'!

We now have 'crony-capitalism' in the USA, where firms and people bribe (with 'donations' to campaigns or Trust Funds and Foundations – ala the corrupt Clintons!) government legislators and executives in exchange for legal or financial benefits. This cronyism damages the economy and our cultural morals and must be stopped before the USA crashes! We are further abused by being an Oligarchy (or Plutocracy), where the wealthiest 1% have broad control.

The **Revolution** will be led by;
1) Our supporters who get elected or appointed to Federal or State positions where they can affect legal and policy issues
2) Supporters who work in the media (TV, Newspapers, Radio, Films, etc.),

3) Book authors who promote many of our principles (new books by Paul Craig Roberts, PhD. and David Stockman are examples; visit Amazon.com), and
4) Activists who sponsor rallies, write articles, and other means of 'spreading the word' (see good work at ActivistPost.com, Antiwar.com, and LewRockwell.com; there are others).

In the Index on P. 219 I include many sub-items (details within a major topic such as Banking, Gold, and Money) I urge you to read them. They all describe 'seldom heard' ideas.

To be legal and effective in the long term, the Revolution changes must comply with our Founders' principles of limited-government, free enterprise, and the Constitution. The Austrian school of thought in economics should be employed (see glossary, p. 211), where individuals and firms make the decisions (within the law), with no government 'management' of the economy and our personal lives.

As shown in the Table of Contents on P. 7, this book offers a collection of my published writings which are all on the Internet, plus others. The intent is to make the writings conveniently accessible in a book (no PC, Portable Device, or Internet needed), and for making margin notes.

Most of our citizens (and in the world) have accepted the immoral and counterproductive attitude that:
1. The government should and will bail out most people and businesses that get in financial trouble, even if due to irresponsible, self-serving, conduct, and
2. It is proper to tax others (typically 'the rich' and 'corporations') to fund benefits for yourself, which I call 'gang-theft-by-vote', or 'charity-by-force'!
Federal money (from taxes, borrowing, or made by the Fed) feeds these bad habits. The Liberals and Progressives want 'their' politicians to fund their projects (to get their votes), but

Object when other politicians support subsidies and favors for the 'capitalism and 'corporations' they hate. Of course, once the door is opened a bit for the government to 'help' and 'manage' social and business projects, it is pushed wide open by these money and favor seekers! The economic and moral decline of our country, and the falling power of our worldwide empire, are the result.

Our monetary system, plus the securities and banking industry are huge factors in implementing the fraud and crony-capitalism that our Revolution will fight. The key issues are:
1. Internationally, the US dollar is the world's primary reserve currency (while this status lasts), so **we are the only nation that can create dollars out of thin air to pay our foreign debts (imports and loans) with our own currency** (most nations must buy US Dollars) without facing exchange rates (very handy for our big spending government !), and
2. Our central bank, the Federal Reserve System, creates new fake money to fund the excessive federal spending (politicians like that better than raising taxes), plus massive bailouts of firms run by their friends, using phony reasons such as 'too big to fail'.

Our massive government spending leads to an excessive increase in our money supply when (as discussed above) create new money to pay our bills!, which causes price inflation and I predict eventual failure of the US dollar as its value drops worldwide.

Thank you for your interest in understanding, and hopefully working to solve, the problems discussed above. If you have questions or suggestions, please contact me at RedickD@aol.com.

****

As proposed above, please help Restore the USA by working to implement our Revolution named 'Forward USA Club'!

First, please join our 'Forward USA Club', by sending me your email address to my address below, and I will put you on the Club newsletter list so we can coordinate our work. I will serve as President of the Club.
The Home page of my blog www.SaferInvesting.org is dedicated to news about the **'Forward USA Club'**. A newsletter, including financial information, will be sent to members monthly.
I need your financial help to cover the cost of printing and sending this book to 'leaders' nationwide, and for other activities to promote the club and achieve our goals. Please send your check (not tax deductible), payable to **'Forward USA',** to PO Box 8432, Madison, WI 53708. Please include return contact info (email is fine). I will deposit all funds in our account at UW Credit Union, Madison, WI. An annual donation of $25 is suggested, which includes a 'Restore..' book. The Clubs' monthly newsletter will document all income and expenses.
My authors' cost for the book is about $ 4, plus about $ 5 for shipping (in to me and out –with a letter- to a 'leader'). An updated book will be sent each year (to refresh their brains) to the President, all Congresspersons and Senators, Governors, Judges, Agency Heads, key staff persons, and candidates. Other 'urgent topic' letters will be mailed, and I will seek appearances as a radio, TV, or seminar speaker, guest, or panel member. Funds are used only for Club expenses. I receive no pay; just expenses. **Thanks.**

If you have questions or suggestions, please contact me at RedickD@aol.com

Thanks and Best regards, Dave Redick

Daves Brief' Bio: (more details on P. 217)

Education; BS-Engineering, Univ. of Michigan, Ann Arbor; MI.
MBA-Economics, Santa Clara Univ., Santa Clara, CA
Work; Aerospace engineer, then sales, and management in
telecommunications. CEO and VP Sales of wireless telcom
consulting engineers HNTelecom.com (closed) in Vancouver,
BC, Canada. Next an entrepreneur as CoFounder/VP of a $6
mill. VC-funded start-up to design/build/operate hi-speed
regional data networks (Search; FiberStreet), based in San
Jose, CA. CEO of SaferInvesting.org.
Political: 'Ron Paul Style' Republican, and Libertarian
candidate for Congress (4 times), and State Legislature
(twice), in CA and WI.
Author: Blog at www.SaferInvesting.org, and since 2009. His
books about government, money, and investing, are all on
Amazon.com.

Chapter 1: Text of Daves' Published Articles

Note: 1) Format for 'Contents Index' below is 'Article # - Page #'- 'A' for in archive.
2) Due to size limitations for this book, the text of some articles is not shown. To see those, use its' link on the Internet. To see my essays on these, and other topics online, go to my archive at ActivistPost.com, scroll to the bottom of the Home page and select 'Contributors', then my name. This will save you typing the link.

Major Topics: (Article Groupings)   Page

****

A. Table of Contents for Articles on 'USA Government Structure & Policies'

(A 'T' after article number means the article text is shown)

 # Page   Title

****

#1) ''The Phases of Empires' ,   Aug-2010

http://www.activistpost.com/2010/08/phases-of-empire.html#more

http://truthiscontagious.com/2010/08/20/the-phases-of-an-empire

http://theburningplatform.com/blog/tag/dave-redick/

http://lewrockwell.com/orig12/redick1.1.1.html , Dec-2011

The Phases of an Empire

The analysis below explains why all empires and "Imperial Style" governments have failed throughout history, and why our Empire-USA faces the same fate. The only question is whether the people and government of the USA have the wisdom and will to engage in a "Managed Decline" by terminating the empire and imperial conduct on their own schedule, rather than by chaotic crash of the US Dollar, economy, and lifestyle. Take notice of the "Solutions" section in Part C below.

Part A: Key Points

-An Empire is a nation that: 1) Owns colonies, and/or 2) Controls, or has great influence over, other nations. Empires require economic and military strength to start and maintain, and this is expensive.

-All Empires fail, and for the same reasons: 1) Expense of military abroad, and subsidies at home. 2) Decline in domestic productivity (spoiled, parasitic citizens). 3) Corruption (illegal conduct) and decadence (unethical and immoral conduct) by leaders and citizens.

-Empire-USA: Our deal to other nations is: we will be the world's policeman and protect you, but you must accept our fake money and "influence." The USA is far into Phase 3-Failure. Look around you for the symptoms shown in Part B-3 and Part C below.

Chart Height Shows Combined Military and Economic Strength (Power and Wealth)

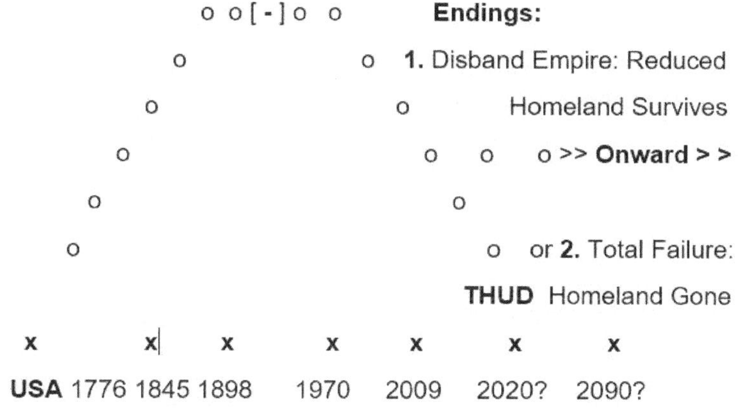

Part B: Events/Symptoms in each Phase

Phase 1 — Growth

-Land: Gain territory by "discovery" (too bad for the natives), or conquest.

-Strength: Start growth of economic and military strength. Sound currency (precious metal, or convertible paper and convertible base-metal coins).

-Government: Local and central government acts as a servant to protect the rights of citizens. No entangling alliances with other nations. New land is governed as a colony or part of homeland nation (becoming a sovereign republic may require a revolution). The army consists of volunteers protecting their homes and families, with no professional or standing army.

-Ethics: Most government people and citizens are hard working and honest. Government is a servant.

Phase 2 — Maturation

-Land: Add contiguous land, or remote colonies, by conquest or negotiation.

-Strength: Become a world leader in both economic and military strength. Homeland receives cheap imports from colonies. Currency is debased to allow more government spending, without raising taxes.

-Government: Grows stronger, more corrupt, and acts as boss, manager, nanny, owner, etc. Elected officials will do almost anything to retain their jobs. Power is used to manage other nations to impose/protect the Empire's interests. The central government increases control (superiority) over local (city and state) functions, often based on its power to create money to fund local projects. A standing army is created and consists of mostly conscripts, and professional careerists. Wars become more oriented to building and defending the Empire.

-Ethics: Corruption and decadence grow due to decline in personal responsibility caused by nanny state.

Phase 3 — Decline and/or Failure

-Land: Lose colonies, or control of other nations, by revolution or voluntary release (due to expense and unrest).

-Strength: No longer a world leader. Power declines by 50% or more, especially in foreign matters. Value of fake currency crashes in purchasing power by 50% or more. Default on debt (or pay off with low value paper money).

-Government: Becomes weak, more corrupt, and desperate. Leaders try to gain power (decrees, martial law, etc.) to survive citizen discontent. "Bread and Circuses" grow, now called grants, subsidies, stimulus, and entitlements. The army consists of mostly professional careerists, and volunteers, many of whom join because they can't find work elsewhere. Standards are lowered (criminal records, non-citizens, health issues) to aid recruiting for wars of empire (non-defense). Use of mercenaries and contractors grows toward 50% or more of total staff, and their loyaty is to their Generals (or Corporate officials), and original homeland, not the country that pays them.

-Ethics: Corruption and decadence are rampant in both social and government conduct. Failure occurs as either: A) Nation survives, but at a reduced level of strength and standard of living (England, France, Italy, Spain, and Russia are examples; see list in Part D), or B) Ceases to exist due to takeover by other nations or groups.

Part C: Empire-USA is in Phase 3: Decline and/or Failure

Problems:

-High Expenses: The expense to maintain bases, and fight wars, worldwide exceeds the monetary and political benefits. The US has over **850 military bases**, with troops (not counting embassies), in over 130 countries, and the US acts as the world's policeman to protect its interests, and impose influence. Resistance by our "subjects" is building. Military expenses are a drag on the economy, and the troops get less than ideal equipment due to cost problems. Host nations are unhappy having our occupying troops.

-High Debt: The US is a bankrupt Empire by any measure. It cannot hope to pay back over $13 trillion in national debt, or the about $50 trillion unfunded future obligations of domestic programs (Medicare, Social Security, etc.). Interest payments are huge. The US Dollar (USD) is still the world's reserve currency (held as if gold by other nations; it can be viewed as a share in USA Inc.), despite the fact that the US is also the world's biggest debtor, but doubts are rising in other countries who use and own dollars for trade. This combination has never occurred before in history! Thus, since all US government debt is denominated in USD, the government can create new low-value dollars out of thin air to pay its debts! A new form of default! The USD is in a precarious position due to excessive expansion of the money supply (inflation) and the USD could crash in value at any time. The extreme is hyperinflation, when the money becomes almost worthless. As with heroin, lots of fake money (the Federal Reserve Bank calls it liquidity) feels good at first, but has withdrawal pain called recession or depression. Since the Federal government never runs out of money, it often becomes the funder for state projects (with strings attached), and states' rights wither. This gives vote-getting power to Congressmen, and acquiescent State officials suck it up to avoid taxing to raise state funds.

-Enemies: The US claims to be a world leader, but this is often a cover to be a bully to control other countries with an occupying force to gain land and resources. This started in 1812 with the failed invasion of Canada, then 1845 with the Mexican-American War, and 1898 with the Spanish-American war (which led to occupation/acquisition of the Philippines and Hawaii). The World Wars, Korea, Vietnam and others followed. The recent Balkans, Afghan, and Iraq wars are primarily about; 1. Control of oil (The US wants it all; no easy-cheap Mideast oil for India and China), 2. Defense of Israel, 3.

Land for bases to control the Mideast, and 4. Continuation of oil sales in US Dollars by Iraq and Iran. The US entered/started all of these wars based on lies by leaders. What a disgrace and ripoff of the people! Trust and respect for the US has declined in the eyes of its citizens and other nations. This meddling foreign policy contributed to 9-11 and terror. The Federal government grasps for new, unconstitutional power.

-Corruption and Bad Ethics: Ethics and social conduct are on the decline in the US. Corruption is rampant in both the government and business. Shady conduct is considered normal (gang theft by vote, "earmark" pork handouts, lying, etc.). Primetime TV is now riddled with sexual content, cursing, glorification of misconduct (The Sopranos, Desperate Housewives, etc.), and violence (NASCAR, cop shows). Sports are riddled with violence (the fans like it!) and cheating, condoned by coaches and team owners that want to sell more tickets. Little or none of the above occurred in the '50s.

SOLUTIONS:

Of the two ways to end the inevitable Phase 3 of an Empire (Decline or Failure), it is far less painful to engage in a "managed decline," or "nation restoration," compared to a massive depression. England and France are examples of 'managed'. A managed process would entail prompt action to:

1. Invoke a major change in foreign policy by: A. Terminating Empire-USA, and its role as policeman and bully of the world, and focus on homeland defense. B. Reducing spending and conflict by closing most, or all, overseas bases, and keeping only a minimal standing army (primarily State-controlled National Guard). C. Stop meddling in the affairs of other nations by force, sanctions, or bribery (no preemptive wars or occupations). D. Promote free trade.

2. Invoke a similar change in domestic policy where: A. Federal spending is reduced by 50% or more. B. Creation

of new fake money is ended. C. Sound money is introduced (paper is convertible to precious metal), and the Federal Reserve System is abolished. D. The Constitution and law are adhered to (with repeal of recent bad laws). E. Market intervention (favors to firms, unions, people) is ended, and free enterprise capitalism (not 'Crony') is used.

These steps would help bring the government back to its proper role to, "**Protect** the personal and property rights of citizens, as individuals, from threat or violation **by others**." With this approach, the USA and its citizens would enjoy a future of peace, prosperity, justice and good ethics. It always works! I cite W. Germany in 1948, and later Ireland, Pr. of Alberta, Can., and New Zealand.

Part D: Empires in History

Name	Start (Phase 1)	End (Phase 3)	Years	Status
Babylonian	1900 bc	1600 bc	300	gone
Assyrian	900 bc	612 bc	288	gone
Carthage	800 bc	100 bc	700	gone
Persian	648 bc	330 bc	318	gone
Athenian-Greek	500 bc	300 bc	200	gone
Macedonian	338 bc	309 bc	29	gone
Chinese	221 bc	1912	233	gone
Roman	27 bc	476-1453	503	gone, split to Byz. & Holy Roman
Byzantine	1054	1453	399	gone
Arabian	630	1258	628	gone
Holy Roman	800	1806	1006	gone
Portuguese	1495	1975	480	Homeland survived
Mongol	1206	1920	714	gone, Mongolia survived
Abyssinian	1270	1974	704	gone
Ottoman	1281	1923	642	gone, Turkey survived
Spanish	1492	1975	483	Homeland survived
British	1500	1950	450	Homeland survived
French	1600	1965	365	Homeland survived
Dutch	1627	1944	317	Homeland survived

Austro-Hung.	1804	1918	114	Austria and Hung. surv'd
USA	1845	(active)	162+	In Ph. 3; #1 world power
German	1884	1918	34	Homeland survived
Japanese	1871	1945	76	Homeland survived

Sources:

1. 'An Inquiry into the Decline and Fall of Nations', W. Playfair, England, 1805 (Rare books library, Toronto, Canada)
2. 'Empire of Debt', Bonner and Wiggins, 2006

****

#2) **''The Cost of Building and Operating Empire-USA'** Aug-2010

http://www.activistpost.com/2010/08/cost-of-building-and-operating-empire.html#more

A Constitutional Republic such as the USA depends on constant vigilance by its citizens to prevent takeover by the always present self-serving power seekers in our midst. Our citizens have become lazy in this regard, and our government's orientation toward empire, spending, corruption, and war are the bitter fruit of this neglect.

We got into our present economic and moral mess in the same way most nations in history have: Corrupt leaders (political and financial) using war, fake money, and debt to enhance their power. In order to get more re-election votes, campaign donations, wealth, and power, it has become "normal" for our leaders and Congresspersons to support: A) Expensive, unconstitutional, programs. B) Counterproductive distortions of the free-market.   C) Non-defense wars for Empire based on lies. Many of their votes in Congress are to serve their friends and campaign donors, not We The People. Our Federal government, and most states, have gone far astray and need to be restored to their proper roles in compliance with their constitutions. States' rights have withered as power, control and funding move to D.C., where the (fake) money is. We have all the traits of **a failing empire** as briefly stated in the three points below.

1, Economics: Our once productive economy has been weakened by fake money (Federal Reserve notes made from thin air, with **no intrinsic value** that allows us to spend like crazy on wars and welfare, and import most of the goods we once made (and thus jobs are exported) so we have become a "consumer economy" using debt for our high life style. Crony-Capitalism and corporate subsidies have replaced free-enterprise and competition. Corruption is routine and rampant.

2, Personal Rights: Our **civil rights** are being voided and abused as government (especially the Feds, who have all the money) and the police act like our boss, rather than our servant as defined by the Constitution. Warrantless wire-tapping, FISA, TSA, absence of habeas corpus, and SWAT teams restricting our right to assemble, are but a few examples.

3, Morals: Our leading faults are: A) The death, maiming and displacement of people, damaging their land with our wars for Empire. B) Our income tax system that is based on gang-theft-by-vote (group A votes to take money from Group B, while the rich to give to Group C: schools, the poor, farmers, pals, etc.). Once the majority of a nation's voters accept this form of taxing through the excuse of "we all benefit," or "make the rich pay their fair share," the door to excess taxation and spending is open, and the government grows like a cancer. Use of progressive rates to increase the percent tax on higher incomes (a penalty on success) adds to the offense. The government is soon viewed as a money pot to do anything nice or needed (the Constitution is ignored), and most people strive for a part of it. Some say, "We need taxes in order to adequately fund our social welfare projects." I say, if you want to help someone, voluntary charity is the best way. It's more work to seek voluntary donations, but it is moral — and less is needed in a prosperous, work-oriented society. No fair using immoral funding methods to support your projects!

For both the economic and moral issues above, an 80% reduction in government spending, and more use of fully compensatory user fees (school tuition, parks, libraries, buses, etc.), would be a good start to needing less tax revenue, and the end of the invasive and damaging IRS.

This would bring a form of free-market pricing (voluntary purchases; no subsidies) to government services: "If people won't pay the full cost (not worth it), don't provide it!" If people really want a service or product, the free-market will always provide it (if allowed by the government!), and history shows the cost to create, operate, and maintain it will be far below what the government cost would be.

Rapid rail transit is a good example. Contractors love to build them (and donate to the legislators who approved them), but ALL of them require subsidies to attract customers, and even so often have low usage. Buses are cheaper and allow more flexible (and adjustable) routing, but don't help politicians get elected! There are a million examples, and they are all dragging us down!

Many of our problems relate to building and operating Empire-USA. We don't own many colonies (territories), but we have a lot of control over other nations, and have over 800 bases worldwide to assure compliance. This is called an "interventionist foreign policy" at best; some would say boss and bully. Empires cost a lot of money to run and also create enemies. People don't like to have foreign troops on their soil, or violations of their culture. They especially hate invading occupiers, hence the attacks on our troops by locals and their insurgent friends. Our bases create a lot of animosity — some violent — as we have seen, with various bombings and 9-11 (see W. Pape's book **Dying to Win**, about suicide bombers; the poor man's nuke). The counterproductive results of Empire-USA are also covered in C. Johnson's three books **The Blowback Trilogy**. Our current economic and military problems are the classic symptoms of an Empire in decline. The original USA was expanded in various ways. The acquisition of land to form what is now the fifty states was done by:

1, Theft by War: A) Land from Spain and France after the expansionary War of 1812 (which we started by invading Canada at Detroit with a goal to annex it), which is now Alabama and Florida. B) Upon winning the 1846 to 1848 Mexican-American War (which started after the guest USA settlers there "annexed" in 1836 the Mexican northern province of Texana, and illegally declared it as the Republic of Texas) we took the northern half of Mexico, now our entire southwest, from TX to CA. C) Annexation of Hawaii in 1898.

2, Purchase: A) The Louisiana Territory from France in 1803 (for $15 mill, 2.8 cents per acre). B) Alaska from Russia in 1867 (for $7.2 mill, 1.9 cents per acre).

3, Negotiation: The Oregon Territory from Spain and England in 1846 — now OR, WA, ID and parts of WY and MT (too bad for the resident 'Indians').

The creation of our overseas Empire and presence started with the Spanish-American War in 1898 (we got the Philippines, Guam and Puerto Rico), and our around-the-world show of strength with Teddy's Great White Fleet from December, 1907, to February, 1909. Our worldwide strength and presence grew while helping the allies win WWI and WW2, both of which we should have stayed out of (Wilson wanted a say in the post-WWI deals, and FDR poked Japan until they reacted at Pearl Harbor so he could get us into WW2 to help his buddy Churchill). These wars allowed us to establish our over 800 bases worldwide, which we now use to control our interests such as oil and economic "cooperation." Maintaining this empire is very expensive due to the cost of foreign bases and foreign aid (bribery), plus occasional wars to expand it (Afghanistan, Iraq, and Iran soon?).

The power of our Executive branch of the Federal government has continued to grow since 1898 because of its accepted role in leading foreign affairs. The fake Gulf of Tonkin incident led to the Vietnam War and LBJ's massive Guns and Butter spending. Then, Nixon abrogated our last monetary connection to gold in 1971, when spending took off even more.

A big increase in executive power was forced by Bush and Cheney, who were the most aggressive in creating an Imperial Presidency, assisted by a meek, self-serving Congress. Long Signing Statements changed laws already passed by Congress! Existing laws and the Constitution were ignored. After their election mandate in 2004, the Democrats took reform off the table, hoping to use the new powers later for themselves (and Obama is!). The Bush-Cheney plan was to rule the USA and the world from D.C., with a focus on controlling access to cheap oil. Pre-emptive wars for economic and political goals (for oil and Israel, not homeland defense), bribes to foreign rulers, domestic pork and welfare, intimidation, assassinations, torture, and sponsored insurrections were their primary tools. The problem with such Imperialistic plans is that they are not only illegal and immoral, but they never work. Expenses, corruption, and backlash/blowback grow faster than the "benefits." Death, and destruction abroad, and a depression, loss of rights, and crushing debt at home, are **the results we see** around us today. Thus, the USA has declined from its peak of military and economic strength in the 1950 – 1970 period, and now faces serious problems. All empires fail in a similar way: A) Corruption and B) Excess spending at home and abroad. Since history, and our own experience, shows that empires eventually do more harm than good to their homeland, it is obviously smart to not be one. England, France, Spain, and Russia had sense enough to back off, and give up their colonies when they faced going broke. The USA should do the same, and emerge as a good customer (with a strong negotiating position) as it enjoys peaceful trade worldwide. This is not a weak or "peacenik" approach, it is the smart way to avoid economic and political failure.

#3) 'How Governments Abuse Our Patriotism', Aug-2010

http://www.activistpost.com/2010/08/how-governments-abuse-our-patriotism.html   Aug-2010

#4T)

http://www.activistpost.com/2010/12/13-lies-abbreviated-history-of-us.html#more

Those of you who long ago figured out that George Bush lied about, and twisted, 9-11, the role of Al-Qaeda, the Taliban, and Osama, and WMDs to justify the invasions of Afghanistan, and Iraq, and to create the War on Terror, will not be surprised to learn that **our prior Presidents, and their complicit henchmen, have lied us into joining or starting every war we have been in since our Revolution. Their true reasons have not been legal, constitutional, or politically acceptable, so they invent one or more false reasons that they can sell to the people**.

The tragic result is that **the USA is the biggest invader and murderer in the history of the world!** Hence my work to change end our policies that 'justify' these world-wide bombings and murders, such as; a) End the gimmick that the USA is the worlds' 'benevolent policeman and guardian' and thus can do 'regime change' or 'nation building' as it pleases, and b) End our unquestioned support of Israel (they control our Congress), which is based on ignoring that Israel was an illegal creation by the UN in 1948, and that they have broken most of the rules of the UN Agreement (invasion and murder in Palestine, and other border 'annexes'), plus their refusal to join the 1968 UN Treaty on the 'Non-Proliferation of Nuclear Weapons', even though the world knows they have a nuclear weapon stockpile, etc.

The recent WikiLeaks disclosures confirm how our foreign policy is riddled with lies. Surprise!

Sadly, most people, especially the troops and their families, believe the lies and proudly support these "wars for defense of our Liberties." It doesn't occur to them that our leaders would be so evil as to spend the lives of our troops to gain their hidden goals for **Empire-USA** (oil, power, land, etc.).

The secret plan of the Bush-Obama gang is to:

A. Take over all oil in the greater mid east (including the east of Caspian 'xxstans', and North Africa), which holds the world's last reserves of easy-cheap oil, so we don't have to share it with China, India, and others

B. Defend Israel at any cost (this helps congressmen and presidents get Israel's AIPAC support for re-election). Control of oil was the hidden reason for the Balkans, Afghan, and Iraq wars.

Iran is their next target

Thus, the war drums are beating in DC to justify bombing Iran, so this is a good time to consider whether our leaders are lying again.

The sole purpose of our military is to defend the homeland from damage or invasion, or a serious threat thereof. It is not for managing world affairs as a global police force, or to build an empire to gain economic or political control of foreign lands and control our "interests" there. Unfortunately, these two missions have been the primary secret agenda for all of our wars since 1898.

Below are the facts on how we got into a few major wars. Each one could be (and has been) a book, and many other smaller wars also could be shown, so please forgive the brevity. The format is: war name; the lying President and the year it started; the stated reasons/lies for the war; and the real reasons.

1. War of 1812 (Madison, 1812) — Lies: In 1812, Congress declared war on England based primarily on their kidnapping ('impressment') of our sailors at sea. Truth: To drive England out of N. America, so the war started with our failed invasion of Canada at Detroit. DC "expansionists" took advantage and started incursions to acquire Spanish Florida, and Mexican Texana territories.

2. Mexican-American (Polk, 1845) — Lies: Fight to defend our Texas border with Mexico. Truth: The disputes started when residents stole The Republic of Texas from Mexico. We invaded and took the northern half of Mexico, now our entire SW region of five states.

3. Civil (Lincoln, 1865) — Lies: Fight to end slavery and preserve the union. **Truth: The South got tired of economic abuse by the North and had a perfect right to secede. It was not a civil war (no plan to take-over the central government) and it was unconstitutional, illegal, and immoral for the North to start a war to stop them**.

The Northern states who had the votes to control Congress, wanted to retain the South as a source of cotton and a customer for their manufactured goods (hence the high tariffs on imports in southern ports). Slavery was partly ended later by the Emancipation Proclamation, but only in Southern states, south of a line along county (not 'State') borders, north of which the Union army was in control. This means slavery continued to be legal in the North (another Lincoln hypocrisy). He made the Proclamation only to free Southern slaves, so the Union Army could recruit them as soldiers. Lincoln was a tyrant beholden to the railroad and canal interests; he jailed journalists and draft resisters who opposed him. Yet, to this day he is revered as a great President who saved the Union. **History shows that the winners always glorify their wars and leaders!**

4. Spanish-American (McKinley, 1898) — Lies: Spain blew up the US battleship Maine in Cuba's Havana harbor. Truth: Hearst publicized, and Teddy Roosevelt mobilized, to use the accidental explosion to take over Cuba by starting a war in April, 1898. We then invaded the Philippines in May and annexed Hawaii in July. A busy time for the beginning of Empire-USA!

5. WWI (Wilson, 1917) — Lies: Join Europe to "Make the World Safe for Democracy." Truth: Wilson was convinced to

join by US and European industrialists who wanted to sell munitions and guns to the allies, and get paid when they won.

6. WWII (FDR, 1941) — Lies; Defend the US from unprovoked attacks by Japan. *TRUTH*: FDR wanted to be sure that Germany didn't win WW2 and become a world power, but joining the war in Europe was strongly opposed by most Americans, so he poked Japan (ended access to oil, scrap metal, etc.) until he got his 'incident' on Dec. 7, 1941 and Congress voted for war. He knew Japan had a mutual-defense pact with Germany so he waited until Germany declared war on the USA on Dec. 11, and hours later he got Congress to declare war upon Germany! FDR wanted the USA to be the only post-war superpower (with 1. Germany under our control, and 2. France and England as buddies)

7. Korean (Truman, 1950) — Lies: Defend America. Truth: Truman and the Generals wanted a reason to have troops in the Far East area of our Empire.

8. Vietnam (Kennedy, Johnson, 1964) — Lies: Johnson said Vietnam attacked our ships in the Gulf of Tonkin in August, 1964. Truth: The US didn't want to lose the southeast Asia region, and its oil and sea lanes, to China. This "attack" was convenient. Kennedy initiated the first major increase in US troops (over 500).

9. Gulf War (G.H.W. Bush, 1991) — Lies: To defend Kuwait from Iraq. Truth: Saddam was a threat to Israel, and we wanted his oil and land for bases.

10. Balkans (Clinton, 1999) — Lies: Prevent Serb killing of Bosnians. Truth: Get the Chinese out of Eastern Europe (remember the "accidental" bombing of their embassy in Belgrade?) so they could not get control of the oil in the Caspian region and Eastward. Control land for bases such as our huge Camp Bondsteel in Kosovo, and for the proposed Trans-Balkan Oil pipeline from the Caspian Sea area to the Albanian port of Valona on the Adriatic Sea.

11. Afghan (G.W. Bush, 2001) — Lies: The Taliban were hiding Osama. Truth: To build a gas/oil pipeline from Turkmenistan and other northern 'xxstan' countries to a warm water (all year) port in the Arabian Sea near Karachi (same reason the Russians were there), plus land for bases.

12. Iraq (G.W. Bush, 2003) — Lies: Stop use of WMDs — whoops, bring Democracy, or whatever. Truth: Oil, defense of Israel, land for permanent bases (we were kicked out of Saudi Arabia) to manage the greater Middle East, restore oil sales in USD (Saddam had changed to Euros).

13. Possible Iran War (Obama, 201?) — Lies: They almost have an atom bomb; they are a threat to Israel; major killer of our troops in Iraq. Truth: Control their oil, defend Israel, and restore oil sales in USD only (they changed to add Euros and others). We created the regional conflict and shouldn't be surprised that all neighbors (including our "friends" in Saudi Arabia) are helping Iraq. We exaggerate the threat to Israel, especially as Iran has allowed inspections and Israel has not.

If you approve of the current Bush-Obama wars, but are resting safely at home, you should join the Army's Chicken Hawk Brigade. There is no restriction on age or sex, and you will get an exciting front-line assignment promptly. Then, you won't feel badly about sending others to fight your wars for oil, religion, and Empire-USA.

Better yet, write, call, and vote against the NeoCon gang in Congress to stop their plans for war against Iran and others.

#5) **'The Role of 9-11 in Middle East Resource Control'**, Jan-2011

http://www.activistpost.com/2011/01/role-of-9-11-in-middle-east-resource.html

#6) **Save the USA by Restoring Gov't to its' Proper Role**, Nov-2012 http://www.activistpost.com/2011/04/save-usa-by-restoring-government-to-its.html#more

#7) **Empire-USA is Crashing: Loss of Power Over Nations Abroad; Broke and Decadent at Home** ',
Sep-2013,
http://www.activistpost.com/2013/09/empire-usa-is-crashing.html#more

#8T) '**Economic and Cultural Decay in the USA**';
July-2014 (updated Aug-2017)
http://www.activistpost.com/2014/07/economic-and-cultural-decay-in-usa.html

Economic Decay
The USA is in the failure phase of Empire-USA. As I note in my analysis of Empires they ALL suffer failure due to; 1) spending and debt cost for the wars needed to grow and maintain the empire, 2) cost of social welfare and business subsidies to keep the people and business managers happy (and help keep the 'leaders' in power), and 3) social decadence due to reliance on government welfare which leads to riots if they are reduced or ended (especially food). Spending and debt for the current "Welfare-Warfare State' has been at dangerous levels since the 1980s. The 'hockey stick; increase started in 1971 when Nixon cancelled the dollar's link to gold. Since then, billions (now trillions) of new dollars were created to pay bills, which creates 'monetary inflation' and reduces the value of the US Dollar (USD).

This fake money has distorted our economy, and excessive imports (paid with newly printed dollars) have caused jobs and factories to be 'off-shored'. Jobless folks are nearing the riot stage as their savings and patience disappear. Sensing this, the Dept. of Homeland Security, and other parts of federal, state and local governments; including the army and police, have stocked-up on guns, ammo, and armored vehicles to fight rioting citizens. It would be better if the governments stopped the riots by not doing the harm described below! The 'leaders' prefer to brand complainers as 'terrorists, traitors, etc.' when they complain about illegal and immoral government acts at home and abroad. I call them Patriots for seeking honest, legal, and moral government. Secrets about illegal acts should be exposed, not protected!
I list below some of the key indicators that we are in decline, will cease being the top world power, and just be 'a medium power' like prior major powers England, France, Spain, and Russia. Most activists agree that China will replace us in our economic, monetary and military dominance.

1. War: As shown in my article about how all of the wars we have started or joined since the 1776 Revolution, were justifieded by lies from the President to serve political and economic goals, not homeland defense. (visit; http://www.activistpost.com/2010/12/13-lies-abbreviated-history-of-us.html#more). The problems and causes of our decline discussed in my Sep. 5, 2013 article (http://www.activistpost.com/2013/09/empire-usa-is-crashing.html#more) have gotten worse, as predicted, and are discussed below.

2. The World's Reserve Currency: Worldwide dominance of the USD started after WW1 (the British pound declined), and escalated with the Bretton Woods world monetary agreement in 1944, which made the USD the 'official' world reserve currency, with gold set at a fixed value of $35 troy ounce. The world's reserve currency is defined as; 1) banks hold it as their reserves; good as gold, and 2) most international transactions use it (USD was 70%, now 60%; yen, Swiss franc, and Euro have most of the rest) as a convenience (saves having many types of currency on hand). Thus, as issuer of the world's primary reserve currency, we are the only nation that can pay its' bills with newly created money. Charles De Gaulle called it our 'exorbitant privilege'. Since 1974, when Kissinger made a deal with the Saudis, all oil has been paid with USD (called 'petrodollars') which has provided support for our fiat USD (no redemption for gold since 1971), but that support, and thus the purchasing power of the USD is fading as nations tire of dealing with the declining value and political rules of the USD.

3. FATCA: A recent big jab was the start of our 'Foreign Account Tax Compliance Act' (FATCA) on July 1, 2014 (and more in July, 2015), which seeks to capture unpaid taxes from US citizens abroad, and imposes a lot of rules, reports, and possible fines, on foreign banks, How arrogant! Many banks are closing accounts of US citizens. They, and private firms, are also working with other nations to use their own currencies to avoid US dominance. This loss of demand for the USD will further reduce it's purchasing power.

Spending and Debt:

Politicians, especially those running empires, need lots of money to pay for wars and benefits to keep business managers (campaign donors) and voters happy. Dictators don't need campaign donations, but they often fail due to riots, or hanging, by angry citizens. Our spending requires massive borrowing, and creation of new money (helped by item 2 above), to pay our bills at home and abroad. Our over $17 trillion in 'admitted' debt (plus unfunded liabilities such as pensions and healthcare, adding about $ 140 tn more!) exceeds our Gross Domestic Product (GDP) by about 5%, which is considered dangerous by any economist. The net interest (after interest income) on our debt is over $500 bill. per year and will soar to disastrous levels when (not if) interest rates increase from our current fake low (1% area) levels.

Summary: How to protect yourself from the above decline: Most Investment Advisors continue to use traditional diversification of stocks, bonds, annuities, maybe some real estate, and ALL are denominated in the falling USD! I wrote this article (http://www.activistpost.com/2013/07/new-factors-in-personal-financial.html#more) to show there are two new elements of diversification; namely currency and legal jurisdiction (nation). Leaving the USD currency and jurisdiction is new to most investors, so requires thought and help. Look at: (http://www.activistpost.com/2014/01/internationalize-to-protect-and-grow.html) for information on how to Internationalize your assets. It will be interesting. Time may be short to avoid the USD collapse, and new US laws that can restrict access to your assets, add more taxes, and even confiscate them! Feel free to contact me at redickD@aol.com, or 608-469-8922 if you have questions. I can supply information, but not investment advice.

Cultural Decay

There is also decline is in the morals of our citizens and leaders. For example it is considered OK by most people to engage in 'gang-theft-by-vote', known as 'tax the rich', to force 'others' pay for your own benefits (subsidized health care and pensions, 'free' K-12 education, unemployment insurance, etc.). They use terms like 'fair share' and 'common good' to justify the forced charity! It should be called 'a penalty on success', or 'gang theft by vote'! Prior to FDR starting social security in 1935, and LBJ starting Medicare in 1965, most people were careful to maintain good relations with friends, family, and the community, because they might need help someday. This meant being honest, polite, reasonably 'normal' in dress and conduct, etc. It also affected personal management of health care as to smoking, alcohol, drugs, and obesity. Now that the government gives people all types of benefits, people have less incentive to be 'respectable', and considerate of others. **They expect to taken care of by the government, and usually are! (by subsidized or free, housing, food, health care, etc.) Most of the receivers of this aid could earn their own way if the handouts weren't available. By making them 'entitlements', the incentive to be self-sufficient is reduced, and most people just line up to collect!** 'Do your own thing' and 'get used to it' were retorts that started in the 1960s. The need for, and pride in, 'personal responsibility' has declined. Now instead of 5 or 10% of our population receiving benefits (largely paid-for by others), we have well over 50% at least partly relying on the government!

Here are a few examples of our cultural decline.

1. Public Morals: In addition to more of traditional immorality such as lying, theft, immodesty, and fraud, we see; 1) more profanity and sex on TV (including family-watching hours; at least the French show it after 10pm), and 2) more fighting and excessive violence in pro sports. It used to be limited to ice hockey, but now we see fights in baseball, and basketball.
2. Personal Appearance

Obesity: Since the 1970s we have seen obesity expand (no pun) in both children and adults. The rapid increase (as to percent of population, and inches of fat) is not just caused by careless over-eating, but also because high-fructose corn syrup, which tends to produce fat, was adopted by bakeries and soft-drink firms because it is now cheaper than traditional sucrose. It is cheaper for two reasons; 1) the government subsidizes farmers to grow corn for production of ethanol fuel, and some is used to produce corn syrup, which is high in fructose, and 2) political import tariffs to increase profits (ie, charge US customers more) of our domestic growers of sugar-cane, and sugar-beets (and get their campaign donations), have made sucrose about twice the world price. This is a classic case of 'unintended consequences' of government meddling, and shows no signs of being terminated (too many donations and votes at stake).

Tattoos and Metal: Widespread (as to both percent of population and body!) wearing of; 1) tattoos and 2) metal pins and rings pierced in any part of one's body, both started in the 1980s. These body deformations were once considered low-class, or embarrassing. I view this conduct as signs that more people don't care what others think of them because it doesn't matter. Of course 'times change' (no more maternity dresses, etc.), but I say these are examples of decline. People now do more weird things because it doesn't matter much what others think of you!

I could add many more items, but I hope the above information makes the point: 'We are a failing empire in both the economic and moral sense'. I show nine links below for articles on this subject by authors I respect. I hope the above article changes the habits of a few people and politicians. Let it be your guide in working and voting for good candidates in the big election coming in Nov-2016!

xxxxxxxxxxxxxxxxxxxxxx

By: David Redick (BS-Eng., MBA-Economics) is an activist for peace and prosperity via better (less) government and free markets. Send comments to redickd@aol.com

Read more at www.activistpost.com; click 'Contributors', scroll to 'Contributing Writers', then alpha to Redick. Also, see more at Part 8 in the left margin of Dave's political site www.Forward-USA.org, and go to the Amazon.com 'books' section to see Dave's books; 'Monetary Revolution USA', 'How to Protect and Grow Your Wealth', and 'Restore the USA'.

1. A Culture of Delusion, by Paul Craig Roberts, Sep 27, 2012 http://www.paulcraigroberts.org/2012/09/27/a-culture-delusion/

2. The 7 Steps You Need to Take to Protect Yourself—and Prosper— During the Coming Economic Meltdown; by Doug Casey , video-2014 http://www.caseyresearch.com/lg/meltdown-video

3. Dead Souls of a Cultural Revolution; by Patrick J. Buchanan, August 23, 2013

4. How Times Have Changed; by Walter E. Williams, July 31, 2012 http://lewrockwell.com/williams-w/w-williams135.html

5. NOTHING TO LOSE; by James Quinn, November 5, 2013 , http://www.theburningplatform.com/ (also see; www.seekingalpha.com)

        Survival Solar Battery Charger - Free Today! (Ad)

6. Challenge to Our Beliefs; By Thomas Sowell www.tsowell.com , December 3, 2013 http://www.lewrockwell.com/2013/12/thomas-sowell/does-the-welfare-state-lower-iqs/

7. The Tribal Mentality; By; Adil Elias, December 03, 2013

http://dollarvigilante.com/blog/2013/12/3/the-tribal-mentality.html

8. The Menace and Immorality of the Welfare State; Prof. Richard Ebeling, Ph.D., Nov. 16, 2009

http://epictimes.com/article/222213/the-menace-and-immorality-of-the-welfare-state http://defenseofcapitalism.blogspot.com/2009/11/menace-and-immorality-of-welfare-state.html7,

9. Gerald Celente, TrendsJournal.com, Nov. 3, 2013 Interview

http://www.thedailybell.com/exclusive-
interviews/34717/Anthony-Wile-Gerald-Celente-on-
Multinationalism-Breaking-the-Chains-and-Individual-
Renaissance/

#9) **'Why the USA is Losing Power, Jobs, and Respect, and Making Enemies'**, Oct-2014

 http://www.activistpost.com/2014/10/why-usa-is-losing-power-jobs-and.html

#10) **'The Real Reasons We Dropped Atom Bombs on Japan'** ,   Aug-2015
http://www.activistpost.com/2015/08/the-real-reasons-we-dropped-atom-bombs-on-japan.html

#11-T) **'Restoration of States Rights and Sound Money are Needed to Help End Decline of the USA'**, Sep-2015

http://www.activistpost.com/2015/09/restoration-of-states-rights-and-sound-money-are-needed-to-end-decline-of-the-usa-econom..html

Introduction

The USA started as a group of English colonies that banded together to reduce oppression and control by the English government, headed by King George III. Various disputes led to the Lexington and Concord gunfights in 1776 which started the Revolutionary War. The Articles of Confederation in 1778 documented the rules and goals of the thirteen sovereign colonies working together. After the war, a Constitutional Convention was convened in1787 to just 'tune-up' the Articles of Confederation and the writing was completed on September 17. They went beyond the tune-up and gave many powers to the federal government. Note that the purpose of this, or any, Constitution is to stipulate what the government may, may not, and must do. It is not a group of laws ('law of the land') but a list of powers granted by the people. The legislature then makes laws within the powers.

When the Constitution was issued to the States for ratification, a major dispute ensued between the Federalist group (likes strong central government, and 'managed economy'; visit **this page**) led by Madison and Hamilton (who wrote the 'Federalist Papers'), and the anti-Federalist group (likes strong State and personal rights; visit **this page**) led by Patrick Henry. Another group, led by George Mason of VA, insisted on ten amendments (the 'Bill of Rights'; to protect the people in case the Federal government exceeded the actual powers granted) to be included before issuing the original Constitution. Twelve were written, and the first ten were ratified. The new Constitution was sent to the states for ratification, and first signed by Delaware on Dec. 7, 1787, and last by Rhode Island on May 29, 1790.

The Growth of Federal Power

More Departments, Agencies, Programs, and Wars: One can present a long list of power functions created by the Federal government (most are unconstitutional), or taken from the States. While it seems clear that national defence, treasury, and international affairs are federal responsibilities (with 'Departments' led by 'Secretaries'), the list has grown to fifteen today including national control with Departments of Agriculture, Commerce, etc., plus hundreds of 'agencies', many of which have unconstitutional rules and police powers (forced compliance, fines, arrests, etc.). See the list **here**. This gives the federal government a monopoly on many aspects of business and personal conduct, and there is an incentive for ambitious, control-oriented, politicians to seek votes with too much regulation and taxes on 'the rich' (or less with big campaign donations!; 'crony capitalism'), while creating welfare entitlement programs for the so-called 'under-privileged' and 'disadvantaged', most of whom caused their own problems. Private charity can handle most of the 'truly needy' with much less cost and fewer side effects. If these programs were run by the States, there would be incentive to treat people and firms with minimal control (low taxes, and regulations) to avoid having them relocate to another State (vote with their feet!). The States would eliminate many programs since they can't create money 'out of thin air', as the Feds do. The damaging effects of the Federal style includes reduced incentive for innovation and work because 'it's not worth it' with high taxes.

Of course only strong governments use war as a tool to gain land and power. The War of 1812 was our first venture, followed by the Mexican-American, Civil, and Spanish-American wars, and many others. These would not have happened if the States were in control. They did not have enough money or power, and it is not likely that a group of states would invade another country. Refer to **this link** about how all of our wars since the Revolution were started on lies, and read below how we used fake money to pay for most of them. Our first overseas war was the Spanish-American war, and since then we have invaded many countries abroad (we now have 900 bases in 130 countries), and murdered thousands of people in the process of building Empire-USA.

Problems caused by paper money made from 'thin air': From its start in 1778, the Federal government has wanted to control the monetary system so as to finance their programs of war and welfare, which are still with us today! The Colonies, and early US states, used many types of currency from other nations, and had no 'official' U.S. money. With the fall to zero value of the paper scrip issued by colonies, and the paper Continentals for the soldiers in the Revolution, the people had learned their lesson about how paper money fails due to creation of excessive quantities, with no redemption for gold. Thus, per article IX, the Articles of Confederation referred to 'value of coin' (thus metallic) as money, and the Constitution went further in Section 10, part 1 by requiring use of gold and silver for coins, made by the States.

To implement these rules, Congress enacted the 'Coinage Act of 1792' (The Mint Act) and established gold and silver as the monetary standards of the United States. The act also allowed for the creation of a national mint. It was the world's first decimal-based monetary system.

Between the adoption of the Constitution and the Civil War the United States government did not issue paper money as we know it today, but on many occasions it did issue short term debt called 'Treasury Notes'.

In 1861 Lincoln needed money to finance the so-called 'Civil War' (actually a war of aggression against the South, which had the right to secede, to retain them as a source of cotton, and a market for Northern manufactured goods), so he got Congress to pass a bill authorizing the printing of full legal tender treasury notes to pay soldiers and buy war goods. The initial 'Greenbacks' were redeemable in gold or silver, but redemption soon ended so the Legal Tender Act of 1862 was issued to force people and firms to accept them. Next came the National Bank Acts of 1863 and 1864 that created a system of federally chartered 'national banks' that issued bank notes. The Acts also put a ten percent tax on state bank notes, which ended their money-making profit so they all quit, which gave us a federal monopoly on money creation! The Secret Service was created, so only DC could safely make counterfeit money! The Federal government finally achieved a monopoly on creation of money!

After several versions of gold and silver money laws, some devious politicians and bankers conspired to get the unconstitutional 'Federal Reserve System' approved on December 23, 1913. It was a true 'central bank' but the politicians knew they couldn't get approval for one, so they gave it a phony name (No use of 'Bank' or 'US'). Its 'mandates' of 'stable value of the USD', and 'full employment' were fake means of getting political and citizen support. Another function was to be 'the lender of last resort' to bailout insolvent banks!! **Remember; 'All central banks are created**

by and for politicians and bankers, so neither runs out of money'. Until FDR ended redemption for people in 1933, the Fed Notes could be redeemed by any owner for gold at $20.67 per ounce. After that, only nations could redeem, but had to pay $35 oz. In the 1960s, many nations worried that we were low on gold so started redeeming in large amounts. We indeed were running out, so Nixon ended redemption on August 15, 1971. Soon thereafter, ALL nations ended redemption. Since then the economic strength of a country has determined the value of its currency, short of excessive monetary inflation. Despite the 'end of gold', the US Dollar (USD), because of our strength, has remained the world's primary 'reserve currency', which means banks hold it for transactions, and most international deals are done in USD. It had been used in 90% of international transactions until our economic breakdown in 2008, and is now about 60%. That decline means other nations are less dependent on us, and may not follow our policies or demands! Many nations, led by China and Russia, are now using their own currencies for deals, which reduces demand for the USD, and thus its' exchange value. Due to monetary inflation (creating new money), and reduced demand, the USD purchasing power has dropped by a factor of ten since 1971, and a factor of 4 since 2000. This means we are heading for an economic cliff much worse than 2008, and must reduce our spending on war and welfare, or CRASH! Table 1 below shows our extreme debt that most officials consider unpayable, but that is their secret!! The staff of all the worlds' central banks are buddies, and playing the same game! The people lose.

Table 1: The Honest National Debt and Unfunded Liabilities

A, $ 19.968 tn National Debt (disclosed debt)

B. 106,985   Key Misc. unfunded Liabilities (not disclosed
     27,792   Medicare A, B, and D (unfunded)
     16,184   Social Security (unfunded)
     ———

$ 150,961 trillion   Total for B

$ 170,929 trillion = Grand Total (A+B)

(Source: USDebtClock.org, Aug. 1, 2017)

Notes for Table 1: 1) Liabilities are unfunded promises based on current tax and funding inputs and on projections using these assumptions and future demographic shifts in U.S. population, 2) National (public) debt is; a. the face or principal amount of all securities (marketable and unmarketable – owned by Fed -) currently outstanding, b. military and civilian pensions, c. retiree health benefits, and d. other guarantees and obligations.
The 'official' government debt figures ignore the above Medicare, Soc. Sec. and Misc. items (treated as 'off-budget' !!), plus potential trillions that loom due to losses at Fannie and Freddie, now government-owned.

What can we do as a nation to avoid the crash, and spare our children and their friends a life near poverty?

My Plan to Avoid the Crash and Achieve More Liberty, Peace and Prosperity

These are the key issues;

1. Use Gold as Money, with no government monopoly: History shows us that when countries use sound money (such as gold coins, or paper and base-metal tokens as redeemable receipts for gold) made by private mints (including banks), and no government monopoly, they have zero or low price inflation, zero or minor 'cycles' of economic panic or depression, and more peace, liberty, and prosperity (smaller governments, less war). The main reason is that the government cannot create

gold 'out of thin air' to pay its bills, and thus must spend less on wars and welfare, etc.! We would expect all countries to use sound money, except the leaders want more money than they can get by just taxing, especially for wars.

Why Gold? All forms of money serve as a 'medium of exchange', 'unit of account', and maybe a 'store of value', which makes it convenient and flexible compared to barter. Think of commodity money as just a step up from barter, but with the flexibility of using it to buy anything. Note that when a valuable commodity (such as gold) is used as money - 'monetization of gold'-, the money has market value (based on demand for industrial and consumer uses) equal to the goods or services in the transaction. Thus it can also be a 'store of value' (savings; keep some for later use), even when not used as money (often called 'intrinsic value').

When gold is used as money, it has no 'price' in dollars, yen, etc. Weight is the unit of account (such as milligrams). Sellers will set prices in weight of gold. There will be prices IN weight of gold, but not OF gold! (Example; What is the price of a dollar?). Gold money will have an 'exchange rate' with other money, but not a 'price'. This will take some getting used to as we evolve to pricing in weight of gold.

To achieve broad use, commodity coins must be made of, or contain, **a material that has these ten characteristics**:

1. Rare, with a low amount in existence now, and limited new supply,

2. Malleable; can be pressed/stamped into coins,

3. Durable; Stable physically and chemically; doesn't break, rust, or rot; can be stored; Tolerates handling,

4. Easy to identify, and determine purity and weight,

5. Difficult or impossible to counterfeit,

6. Homogeneous; a piece is the same throughout,

7. Divisible into pieces; diamonds and pearls aren't,

8. High value per ounce; not bulky to handle or store,

9. Acceptable to most Sellers; familiar and saleable,

10. Has market value when not used as money. Thus; a. is equal in value to the items in a transaction, and b. is a store and measure of value.

The 'market' (users of money; not governments or habit) has decided that gold fits these requirements best, but silver and copper can have a role in parallel, with no fixed ratios set as to value per gram (i.e., no bi-metallic standard). The coins must be valued and marked by weight of their precious metal content (such as 'milligrams'), or the amount they can be redeemed for.

There is always 'enough' gold for money, because if a nation's economy (GDP) grows faster than its gold supply, the increased demand will cause their gold for domestic transactions to **APPRECIATE** in purchasing power per ounce, which in turn cause deflation (lower prices). The same logic applies to the world economy. It is self-adjusting and needs no government meddling!

The conversion from Fed Notes to 'Gold as money' would entail dividing our money supply (M3, including Treasuries) into the ounces of gold we own (the Fed claims 8,134 tonnes, but is probably much less). Under the present system, this would value gold at about $55,000 per troy ounce. Upon conversion, each USD would be redeemable for a tiny amount of gold, as calculated above. This would eliminate any 'run' to get rid of one's USD before conversion. Later, a new currency would be issued to replace the Fed Notes. See more detail in my book *MONETARY REVOLUTION USA* from Amazon.com.

2. Restore the Power taken from the States

As discussed in the Introduction above, our nation started with the States having considerable power, but they have been stripped of much of it over the years. In some cases (highways, welfare, medical, etc.) they give it up in exchange for money for Federal subsidies of state functions (maybe some votes too!).

a) An obvious first step is to revise amendment 16 of the Constitution to limit or end Federal income taxes. A low flat tax or sales tax could be the answer.

b) Restore amendment 17 of the Constitution, which will again allow the States to appoint the US Senators, thus representing State interests.

c) A more complex step is to give the States more direct power over the federal government. (even more than in the original constitution). I suggest we copy the Canton system in Switzerland. The Cantons can vote to void a federal law, or terminate a legislator. This keeps the central government legislators giving priority to the people rather than themselves!

Space does not allow discussion of Medicare, Medicaid, Social Security, Immigration, etc., but these need to be considered in any final plan.

Summary

I don't underestimate the difficulty of, and opposition to, a transition to gold as money, and restoring power to the States. Some will say we should set less ambitious goals, but I say these lesser goals are just steps along the way and we must never stop striving for the ultimate goal of reducing harmful government spending and control.

Maybe if we hit bottom hard enough (2020, 2030?) in the current recession, people and the government will start to listen to us.

#12) **'Why Save Empire USA'; The Elites Need It!**
Aug-2016;

An empire is the ultimate source of power and money for politicians, war-goods producers, and the military. An empire exists when a nation owns or controls other nations or lands. Empires have been rising and falling since the Babylonian empire started in 1,900 BC. It lasted 300 years. There have been 22 more since then, but only one, 'Empire-USA', exists today. For details, see my article on empires at item 1) above.

Our political, business, and military 'leaders' have gone from concern in the 1990s, to panic since 2005, about the rapid decline of our world-wide economic and military superiority and control. They want an enemy and some action, and will create them with proxy/fake events as needed! This article shows how most of the 'big-government' changes in the last ten years are related to boosting their power, and making the citizens more docile and defenseless. For example, citizens' rights and conduct are subdued by the TSA, police abuses, and gun controls.

The Growth of 'Empire-USA'

The USA has been building an Empire since the 'War of 1812' when Pres. Madison tried to force England out of North America by invading and annexing Canada, but failed due to lack of citizen support. However, the U.S. finally won in 1815 and signed the 'Treaty of Ghent', which was a friendly settlement with no changes of territory, and gained us recognition as a 'real' country in world politics (not just a bunch of revolutionaries). The next large action was the 1845 'Mexican American War' where we stole the northern half of Mexico (from TX to northern CA). For a list of wars for empire (not defense) see my article **here**. When England and France were weakened by the expense and damage of WW1, the USA emerged as a financial power, with the US Dollar (USD) the de facto primary world reserve currency. It was formalized in the 1944 Bretton Woods agreement and the USD was then used in about 70% of international transactions! This status allows us to create new money to pay our bills (any Seller will accept it). French leaders called this an 'exorbitant privilege', and it was! Since then we have expanded our money supply so much that the 'purchasing power' (how many apples a $ will buy, etc.) has dropped by over 95% since the Federal Reserve System started in 1913. Thus items priced in USD have gone up! Our trading partners became concerned about decline of the USD and in the mid-1960s England and France began exchanging paper dollars for our gold (redemption). We were running out of gold so Pres. Nixon ended redemption Aug-1971. The USD became 'fiat' (worth what the government decrees, enforced by 'legal tender' laws), and the world followed. Whoopee, every nation could make money out of thin air, and we led them all with Fed-based 'monetary inflation', followed by market-based 'price inflation'. As the world's leading economic and military power, Sellers continued to accept our USD, but at a constantly declining value (as we continued to create more). The effect on pricing is shown by the price of a family car going from $2,000 in the 1970s to $20,000 in 2000, and a room in Motel 6 from $6 to $50!

Since the 1990s, other major nations (and their private banks and firms) have started to avoid using or holding the USD, and now often use their own currencies for international transactions. Examples are; 1) The BRICS (Brazil, Russia, China, India and South Africa), 2) China bought a large amount of oil and gas from Russia, denominated in Yuan, 3) Russia is forming the 'Eurasian Union', and 4) China's 'Asian Infrastructure Investment Bank' (AIIB), attracted members worldwide (including our 'friends' England and France), and are challenging the US control of world banking, and the USD status as the world's primary reserve currency.

In addition, they have started their own **international bank-clearing network** to avoid reliance on the current SWIFT network (Society for Worldwide Interbank Financial Telecommunication), which is managed/controlled by the USA. As a result, the USD has fallen to use in only about 50% of international transactions, and thus our power to control foreign affairs with monetary and banking sanctions has declined. 'On Oct. 1, 2016 the IMF plans to include the Chinese Yuan in their inter-government money called 'Special Drawing Rights' (SDR, see article on p. 81). This is a big boost to the Yuan's value and credibility, and will reduce, the amount of USD per SDR. This will lower the power and value of the USD when used alone, and some analysts predict will reduce the price of all stocks, etc. denominated in USD (due to lower demand), and increase the price of precious metals.

We are far into the Empire failure mode as described in Phase 3 below. As we continue to decline in political and economic power, our control of international events will decline until we are not a major factor. This is what happened to France and England after WW1, and many other Empires before.

How Empires Grow and Fail

The following Phases show four key characteristics that vary as empires build, grow and fail. Note that all empires fail. The USA must purposely end Empire-USA by invoking a non-interventionist foreign policy, and end other 'control' and 'mutual defense' entanglements, or it will fail the hard way!

Phase 1 – Growth (shown on chart below)

* Land: Gain initial Homeland territory by 'discovery' (too bad for the natives), or conquest.

* Strength: Start growth of economic, political, and military strength. Sound money (coins made of precious metal, plus redeemable paper notes; Private mints; No central bank).

* Government: Initial type can be anything; Democracy, Socialism, Communism, Monarchy, etc.

* Ethics: Most government people and citizens are hard-working and honest. Government is a 'servant'.

Phase 2 – Maturation

* Land: Add contiguous land, or remote colonies, by conquest, annexation (Hawaii), or negotiation.

* Strength: Become a world leader in economic, political, and military strength. Homeland receives cheap imports from colonies. Currency is debased (base metals added, or weight reduced) to allow government spending, without raising taxes.

* Government: Grows stronger and acts as boss, manager, nanny, owner, etc. Power is used to 'manage and control' other nations to impose/protect the Empire's 'interests'.

* Ethics: Corruption and decadence grow; 1) In government, due to increased power and arrogance, and 2) In citizens, due to decline in personal responsibility caused by nanny state.

Chart 1: The Phases of an Empire

Chart Height Shows Combined Political, Military and Economic Strength (Power and Wealth)

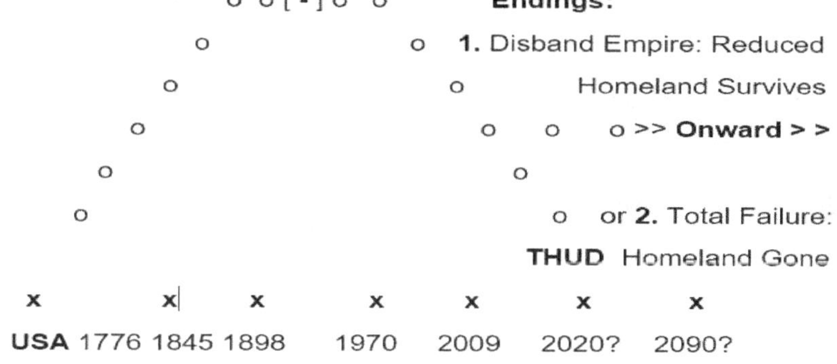

Phase 1, Growth – Phase 2, Mature – Phase 3, Decline or Fail

* Land: Lose colonies (or control of other nations) by revolution or voluntary release (due to expense and unrest).

* Strength: No longer a world leader. Power declines by 50% or more. Value of fake currency crashes in purchasing power by 50% or more. Default on debt (or pay-off with low value paper currency).
* Government: Gets weak and desperate. Leaders try to gain power to survive citizen discontent. Roman-style 'Bread and Circuses' grow, now called grants, subsidies, stimulus, and entitlements. Government controls, and 'tough' police tactics make citizens more submissive.
* Ethics: Corruption and decadence are rampant in both social and government conduct.

Failure occurs as either; A. The Nation survives, but at a reduced level of strength and standard of living (England, France, Italy, Spain, and Russia are examples), or B. Ceases to exist due to takeover by other nations or groups.

Solution

The self-serving politicians, generals, and business leaders fight the decline in their favorite way; More War and Controls. That keeps their salaries and orders coming, but does not solve the problem of economic failure we face. They keep troops in NATO (and pay for most of it; thus we are the Boss!) and the far-east. We have troops at more than 180 bases in over 100 countries! We must remember that use of violence trickles down from military to people and police (for militarized homeland police, the citizens become the enemy), which results in Blowback in the form of terrorists and refugees overseas, and more riots and cop-killers at home.

As Justin Raimondo said (**AntiWar.com**, 6Aug2016);

"The age-old scam of governments creating problems that they then use as an excuse to increase their powers so they can "solve" them is on full display in Libya – and Syria, and Iraq. All these countries had secular governments where not a trace of Islamist radicalism could be found. Their "liberation" by the Western powers, who launched regime change operations in the name of "democracy," gave rise to ISIS – and created the rationale for yet more destructive intervention."

Citizens of the USA need to fight for a return to the limited constitutional powers granted to our government by the people. Then there will be no wars by Presidential decree, our spending will be limited by return to the gold standard, and economic growth will blossom.

We citizens need to stand up and fight the big-spending 'Establishment', and their illegal and immoral wars for economic and political goals (not defense), or they will spend and bomb the USA into economic, moral, and social failure. They don't care about failure of the US economy, and the social damage caused, because they will be in a villa on a nice island somewhere!

If you have read this far you must be interested, so I suggest you DO SOMETHING such as support a candidate for Congress or President that will fight for us. There are many other ways. (Aug-2016 Insert; Refer to p. 12 and 199 to join the **'Forward USA Club'**, and make a donation.)

Thanks, and good luck.

****

Blank

B. Text of articles, and book excerpts, about 'Monetary Systems'

Article Contents: (# followed by a 'T' means the text is shown, and 'A' if in archives.). To see my essays on these, and other topics online, go to my archive at ActivistPost.com, scroll to the bottom of the Home page and select 'Contributors', then my name. This will save you typing the link

\#   Page   Title

1T-59-A **Why Use Gold as Money?**

2T-63-A **How to Abolish the Fed and Convert to Gold as Money**

3T-71 **Excessive Spending, Taxation, and Controls are Destroying the U.S. Economy'**

4-70-A **The Impact of Fiat Money as the World's Reserve Currency'**

5-71-A **Convert the USA Monetary System to Gold**

6-72-A **Germany Should Quit the Euro & Use Gold As Money**

7-72-A **Will Basel III Allow Gold Money to Prevent a Crash of the USA Economy?**

8T-72-A **The U.S. Government and Consumers are Big Spenders Heading for a Crash**

9-77-A **The Key Factors in a Sustainable Gold Standard for Money**

10-77-A **A Plan to Convert the US Dollar to Gold as Money**

11T-77 **'Benefits of a Gold Money World'**, from Daves' book; 'Monetary Revolution USA' , p. 140

****

#1) Why Use Gold as Money? , Dec-2010

http://www.activistpost.com/2010/12/why-use-gold-as-money.html

History shows us that when countries use a valuable commodity for money they have zero or low inflation; zero or minor cycles of economic panic or depression; and more peace, liberty, and prosperity (smaller governments).

For example, the number of grams of gold needed to buy a barrel of oil has been very steady over the years. A key benefit of using gold as money is its value stability. Even better, Econ 101 tells us that a commodity such as gold in limited supply, and with increasing demand for it (growth of the economy), will **APPRECIATE** in value. This has huge importance because it kills the "there is not enough gold" argument, and gives a positive incentive to save and avoid debt.

Thus, we would expect all countries to use sound money, except the politicians want more money than they can get by just taxing, especially for wars. They want a way to create money "out of thin air." Fiat money ("face value" decreed by the government, not redeemable for gold; we call ours Federal Reserve Notes) serves this purpose. Even when some level of redeemability (exchange for precious metal) exists, governments often suspend it before, during, and after wars, which the US did for the Revolutionary, 1812 and Civil wars, after which it must be pushed to restore it — often with less value.

The two key reasons for using a commodity as money are to:
A. Limit excess expansion of the money supply (inflation; loss of value) by the government (you can't trust them).
B. Provide a market-based store of value. The commodity could be wheat, iron, diamonds, or pearls, but the market (users of money) usually chooses gold because it works best.

To achieve broad use, **commodity coins must be made of, or contain**, a material that is:
1) Rare, with a low amount in existence now and limited new supply.
2) Malleable, so can be made into coins.
3) Stable physically and chemically; doesn't break, rust, or rot (can be stored; lasts through much handling).
4) Easy to identify (recognize), and determine purity and amount.
5) Difficult or impossible to counterfeit.
6) Homogeneous in content (a melted chunk is the same throughout).
7) Divisible into pieces (diamonds and pearls aren't).
8) High value per ounce (not bulky to handle or store).
9) Acceptable to most sellers (familiar and recognizable).

10) Has market value when not used as money. Thus; a. is equal in value to the items in a transaction, and b. is a store and measure of value.

This approach allows the use of representative paper notes ("claim checks" for gold), or base-metal tokens, so long as they are marked to show the amount of gold they can be redeemed for by any bearer, on demand.

The market of money users has decided that gold fits the above requirements best, but silver and copper can have a role in parallel, with no fixed ratios set between them as to value per gram (i.e., no bi-metallic standard). It is interesting to note that gold is not "consumed" as are other commodities, including silver and copper. Thus, except for wear, over 90% of all gold mined in history still exists (even if buried in a tomb). Silver and copper supplies and costs are more volatile than gold (more new production, are consumed for industrial use, etc.), so are less attractive, but usable. When gold is used as money, it has no "price" anymore — weight is the unit of account. This will take some getting used to as we evolve to pricing in weight of gold.

History

From its origin until 1913, the US used a combination of foreign and domestic coins and local "bills of credit," had two failed central banks, Continental and Greenback paper dollars (both became worthless), and various runs and panics in a turbulent banking system. The unconstitutional Federal Reserve System was created in 1913 and had a monopoly on creation of "legal tender" money. It was secretly planned by bankers and politicians, for bankers and politicians. At first, anyone had the right to trade-in their Silver Certificate paper dollars for a silver dollar (this ended in 1968), and deal in gold for transactions. In March, 1933 (his first month in office) FDR took those rights from mere people, and only nations could redeem paper for gold. In 1971 Nixon ended this right for nations when he abrogated the 1944 Bretton Woods Agreement due to our serious financial problems (a. We were running out of gold because France, England, and others were redeeming the US dollars accumulated in Europe due to our postwar spending and loans there, and b. The US was poor after spending on Vietnam and LBJ's 'Great Society', etc.). With no link to gold, the US could make dollars out of thin air as needed, and did we ever! Prices started their 'hockey stick' shaped rise a few years later as the effect of excess money creation and spending trickled to the world economy. Within in a few years, all nations worldwide ceased redeemability, even the prudent Swiss floated the Swiss franc (SF), but have been less abusive than others; hence while 1 US$ = about 4 SF in 1961, it is now about 1 US = 1 SF, so they only inflated by 2.5 while by 2008 the US inflated by 10; 4 times more!

Where We Are Today

The US has been the worst abuser among developed nations (older countries remembered their lessons from past monetary failures). The US has created so much new free, fake money since 1971 that the US dollar has lost about 80% of its purchasing power since then (this excess expansion of the money supply is called monetary inflation, like a balloon) with its consequent price increases (due to loss of the dollar's purchasing power) called price inflation. Check prices of common commodity items (that are not imported, subsidized, cheaper due to new technology, or under price control), such as a pizza, a restaurant meal, or even a car. Good examples are:

1. A room at a Motel 6 cost $6 in the 1950s, but is now in the $50 range in 2010 (same type of room and service)
2. A family car cost about $2,000 in the '60s, but is now about $20,000 in 2010.

There is your 8 to 10X loss of USD value since the late 1940s (when the post-war big-spending started)! This ties-in with the over 95% loss of the dollars value since the Fed started! The only reason we can get away with our worldwide spending and borrowing is because the USD is the world's reserve currency (any person or bank will take and keep it as if "good as gold") and we can create new money to pay our bills. The dollar is viewed as a share in USA, Inc., the world's strongest economy, which sadly is fading (faster since 2007), as we continue the long abuse of our economy (by spending, taxing, and harmful intervention by the Fed and government) and money (by excess expansion of the supply). The era of US world dominance is ending, as it does with all empires (Rome, Spain, England, France, etc.). When (not if) the dollar loses its reserve currency status, there will be a 50% or more loss in value in a few days, and prices at Wal-Mart will triple!

Politicians and bankers love an unending supply of cheap money, but such fiat systems always fail. It is part of the pattern for all failed empires in history, and the **Empire-USA** is now entering the failure phase. To avoid a chaotic crash, we must reduce spending (including our role as the world's policemen and bully), and convert to a gold-money system! The gold we own could be used to back all existing US dollars, and allow redemption of paper for gold. This would amount to about 2/10,000 ounce per dollar (or less if the Fed is lying about how much we have), and imply a price of about $50,000 per ounce. Thereafter, prices would be in weight of gold (grams, milligrams). All nations would soon convert to gold money, or sellers would not accept their trash paper. Variable foreign exchange valuations would end between countries using gold. The IMF, World Bank, BIS, G-20, and all other meddling government groups would fade and die (good). Time is short (1 to 10 years) before the big crash starts.

Write, call and visit your Senate and Congress persons to urge support of this new system. Most now prefer hyperinflation (print money to pay bills), or default (ignore debts), but that causes more damage and has no future benefit. Despite the pain and losses the conversion to gold may cause, the damage is far less than an uncontrolled crash, and there is a bright future afterward. Let's get started

#2) How to Abolish the Fed and Convert to Gold as Money ,   Jan-2011

 http://www.activistpost.com/2011/01/how-to-abolish-fed-and-convert-to-gold.html#

The House Financial Services Subcommittee, which provides congressional oversight of our central bank, the Federal Reserve System (Fed), the managers at the Fed are facing the dreaded time when they may have to reveal the secret dealings that they use to help their political and banking friends worldwide.

Vanity and job security are a big part of what guides Fed managers. They love the power and prestige of their jobs, and do whatever is needed to please the politicians who put them there. Of course, most of them are 'true believers' in the need for their control of 'monetary policy', despite the horrible record of the Fed, which has caused the US Dollar to lose over 95% of its value (purchasing power) causing prices to rise (price inflation) since the illegal, unconstitutional, creation of the Fed in 1913. The main reason for this decline is expansion of the money supply (monetary inflation) caused by creation of fake 'fiat' money; where 'face value' is decreed by the government, even though the material it is made of may have more or less market value.

Most countries have central banks, but ours is the only one that is a private corporation owned by other banks; more on that below. Rep. Paul has made his concerns and solutions clear in his popular September, 2009 book *End the Fed*, as I have in my December, 2010 book *Monetary Revolution-USA*. As in these books, this essay will show why sound money (coins made of, or paper backed by, a commodity such as gold or silver) ends the so-called need (and means) for the counter-productive meddling of 'monetary policy' and fake money by the Fed in our nation's economy.

The first salvo in their fight for survival was an article by Paul Hobby (Chairman of the Houston branch of the Dallas Fed) **Hands Off the Fed** in the Houston Chronicle on Jan. 22, 2011. In his defense of the Fed from expected criticism by Rep. Paul, he said, 'No one who studies the global economic issues today would forfeit this nation's ability to conduct monetary policy through a central bank', and 'Because the dollar is a fiat currency, confidence is the only backstop, and aggressive monetary policy provided that confidence at a decisive moment.' Kudos to Robert Wenzel for his January 23, 2011 article **Is This the Best the Fed Can Do in Its Defense?** where he challenges Hobby's article and describes the false statements and counterproductive conduct by the Fed.

I say, yes indeed our 'Fed Notes' (dollars) and base-metal coins are 'Fiat and based on confidence', and that's why we have the FDIC (Federal Deposit Insurance Corp.) to give depositors false 'confidence'. With sound money, no FDIC, central bank, or legal-tender laws are needed, and poorly managed banks are subject to insolvency and bankruptcy. No more bailing-out of greedy bankers (also political buddies) who use high-risk deals and high-leverage fractional reserves to increase profits. The sound money approach produces more personal responsibility by depositors to keep an eye on their bank and move their deposits to another one if they don't like its policies. The incentives are positive for both the depositor and bankers. We now have 'nanny' government serving this watchdog role, which creates the corruption and failure we see around us today.

Creation of the Fed
Politicians and bankers like central banks that control the national monetary system, because they can manipulate them to gain funding (create money) without politically unpopular taxation. England created the world's first central bank in 1694. In 1791, the 'First Bank of the United States', (BUS-1), was started, but it failed in 1811. The second attempt was the 'Second Bank of the United States' (BUS-2), which was chartered in 1816, with a renewal required in 1836. The main reason that BUS-2 was chartered was that spending for the War of 1812 caused severe inflation and we had difficulty in financing military operations. It was a privately held corporation that had privileges with the federal government to give it access to substantial profits. President Andrew Jackson strongly opposed the renewal of the bank's charter, and built his platform for the election of 1832 around doing away it, which he did in Sep-1833. The Federal Reserve System should be considered the third U.S. central bank (BUS-3). The plan to create this financial monster was consummated on November 22, 1910 in a secret meeting at a private club on **Jekyll Island, Georgia**.

This meeting included seven of the most powerful financial people in Europe and America, led by Sen. Nelson W. Aldrich, who was a business associate of J. P. Morgan and father-in-law to John D. Rockefeller, Jr. The sole intention of these conspirators was to draft a blueprint for a strong central bank that served their interests. This was the blueprint for the Federal Reserve System and the prize was the future control of the money supply and credit of the United States. It was created 'By Politicians and Bankers, for Politicians and Bankers'.

Because the Federal Reserve System was authorized to issue paper money (first 'Silver Certificates', then 'Federal Notes'), it was unconstitutional from its inception because Article 1, Section 8 of the Constitution only allows the government to 'coin money', and further does not permit it to create and operate a bank. Another challenge to the schemers was to prepare a program of fundamental banking reform and get it past the scrutiny of patriotic Congressmen and the American public.

Aldrich headed a commission in 1911 to study the role and need for central banks. He came home from a study trip to Europe claiming to be a new supporter of them, but that was a ploy to cover the existing plans from Jekyll Island in 1910. The Aldrich Commission's report was submitted to Congress in 1912. Although Woodrow Wilson, a Democrat, won the 1912 election, the Republican Aldrich's plan shaped the extensive debate that followed. A Democrat, Carter Glass of Virginia, shepherded the Federal Reserve Act through the Congress. On Dec. 23, 1913, when many Congresspersons, including major opponents of central banking, had already left town, Congress adopted the Federal Reserve Act, also known as the Owens-Carter Act.

Even the name was meant to deceive, so they chose: 1. 'Federal' to make it seem to be part of the government, and 2. 'System' instead of 'Bank' because many Congresspersons opposed a federal bank. They planned the 'system' with twelve regional banks (each a privately owned corporation) to satisfy private bankers that their regional concerns would be heard.

Some people claim the above 'secret meeting' never happened, but one of the group, Frank Vanderlip, wrote a first-hand account of the meeting a quarter of a century later (1935) in his book *From Farm Boy to Financier* (out of print). Thus, the Fed was created, and was assigned twin policy goals of; 1. Price stability, and 2. Full employment. It has been an extreme failure at both, as described below. Of course, as a government body, this failure is not seen as a reason to restructure or abolish it! The Politicians and Bankers still want it as a means to create money out of thin air!

The Fed's Record of Results
The purchasing power of the US dollar has dropped by more than 95% since the Fed started in 1913, all due to excess creation of new money (expansion of the money supply; monetary inflation). This hurts the people (especially those on limited or fixed incomes, and those with savings), but the bankers have done well, since they make money selling US debt (T-bills, etc.) and get bailed-out when in trouble due to their own greed (Bear-Stearns in 2008, etc.). Most Fed meetings are secret, and proceedings are not even available to Congress. Preposterous! Some economists say the Fed is needed in order to assure adequate 'liquidity' or 'elasticity' for growth by proper expansion of the money supply, equal to growth of the economy; about 3 to 5% per year. The problem is that such powers are *always* abused by governments (by expansion of 10 to 20% per year, or more!), though some (the Swiss) less than others (the US is among the worst of the major currencies).

We cannot, and should not, trust the government or Fed to 'manage' our monetary system. This excess money causes bad spending and investment decisions at both the business and personal level, which creates financial distortions (big peaks, then valleys), as seen in: 1. Bailing-out England after WW1, leading to mal-investment (too much money around) and the crash of 1929 when the Fed suddenly reduced the money supply by about 30%, and 2. The 2007-2008 housing price and construction collapse due to a Fed interest rate increase of 4.25% (from 1 to 5.25%) in 2006, and 3. Many other large peaks and valleys, and 90% loss of purchasing value, since the Fed was created. So much for government 'management' of currency and the economy!

What Should We Do Now?
Our present system of big spending and fake money is not

sustainable. The Fed should be abolished and Fed Notes replaced by gold as money. This will; 1. Put limits on government spending by stopping its endless supply of fake money, and 2. Reduce or end the wars and business cycles funded by it. The use of gold as money gives a positive incentive to save, and avoid debt, due to *appreciation* of purchasing power of the money. Econ 101 tells us that a commodity (such as gold) in limited supply, and with increasing demand for it (growth of the economy), will *appreciate* in value. This has huge importance because it kills the 'there is not enough gold' argument against gold! Appreciation is ignored by most economists and suppressed by, or unknown to, all politicians. The conversion of our present Fed Notes to 'gold as money' can be done by the following 'Six-Step Plan' (this is a 'short-form' description).

Step 1 Repeal all legal tender laws so private firms (mints) can issue new money. The Federal Reserve will be abolished five years after private money becomes legal (or if Congress refuses abolishment, let it atrophy to death from lack of customers and income).

Step 2 Allow private mints to be created without government permission or license, with new gold money labeled by the weight of gold a coin contains, or that tokens or paper certificates represent.

Step 3 Require the Federal Reserve banks, the U.S. Treasury (Ft. Knox), the Exchange Stabilization Fund, and any other part of the United States government, to promptly submit to a private audit of the amount and quality of gold they own and its title status (leased?), reveal the results to the public, and then give it all to a 'Redemption Trust' owned by the U.S. Treasury, to be used to redeem existing coin or paper currency on demand, based on a certain weight per Dollar, in accordance with the plan below. Private sources put our total money supply (M3) at about $14 trillion worldwide in mid 2010. If the M3 dollars were redeemable in our claimed 260.415 million troy ounces of gold there would be 0.0000186 oz. per dollar. This means 53,763 dollars would equal one troy ounce, thus an ounce would be worth $53,763, in today's pricing method. This implies a 97% drop in the dollar's current value versus today's $1,400 per oz. The dreaded day of reckoning! But this issue fades as all nations convert to gold money, and they must, or no sellers will take their trash 'money' once the US dollar is redeemable. There will be no 'price' for gold, just its weight.

Until a proper audit is done, we cannot be certain how much gold the US has. Fortunately, the amount of gold per dollar is not crucial. It will set a new standard, whatever it may be, and we will grow from there. The same applies to all nations that also convert. There will be no 'price' for gold, just its weight. Thus, sellers will show prices of things by weight of gold (food, cars, whatever), such as '20 milligrams' each, etc. People and governments may want to assign a 'name' to certain weights (that's how the 'dollar' got started, as a weight of silver), but this should be avoided because it leads to corruption by reducing the weight or quality of the metal associated with a 'name, and the 'name' is then used in pricing. This is called 'debasement' of the currency; an old story since before the Roman Empire.

Step 4 Abolish the unconstitutional GSEs such as Fannie, Freddie, Ginnie, and Sallie Mae, FHA, Pension Benefit Guaranty Corp (PBGC), FDIC, all TARP-Like projects, 'special' bankruptcies, corporate-takeovers, Recovery-Stimulant Acts, the Exchange Stabilization Fund (ESF), the Export-Import Bank, etc., etc. All of these are part of the government's intervention in, and manipulation of, money, private business, and banking.

Step 5 Terminate US membership in the IMF (and get our gold back), World Bank, BIS, G-20, G-8, United Nations, and others. Their 'manipulation' role will end with use of money valued in weight of gold. Free trade and embassies are adequate for communication with other nations.

Step 6 Work to repeal or change other unconstitutional and counterproductive Federal laws, and policies that intervene in our lives, economy, and the world.

The above 'Six-Step Plan' includes a formidable list of legal changes, and of course most people in government (all branches, and all levels; city to federal) will oppose them, initially. However, as our economy and the US dollar crash (2012, 2020 ??), the pressure for change will be enormous, and we will win many converts to gold. An advantage of this plan is that just the removal of legal tender laws will allow gold money to prove its benefits. Other changes can follow. Central bankers and the IMF are already devising methods to minimize damage from the dollar's ongoing decline. The current plan is to use a 'basket of currencies', including the USD, Yen, Euro, and Yuan. they hope this will allow a 'graceful decline' of the USD as the world's reserve currency, without wreaking havoc and losses in world banking and commerce. It won't work, because they will still end up using fiat money manipulated by politicians and bankers.

As painful as this transition to 'gold as money' may be, it is better than the hyperinflation (with currency values approaching zero) that is otherwise 99% likely to occur.

We can enjoy the benefits of sound money, and avoid a crash of our economy, currency and lifestyle if we implement this plan for conversion to gold money. If we crash, meaning severe reduction in economic activity (depression), and 50% to 90% loss of purchasing power of the US dollar, we will need to rebuild from the ashes. This can be viewed as an opportunity for the people to spontaneously start using gold as money. They will see its benefits, and demand to keep it! The laws can follow. Politicians will be desperate to keep their jobs so will cooperate to pass and repeal laws as needed; otherwise they will be fired and replaced.

It will require something like the above 'crash' circumstances, and a people-led Monetary Revolution, to take back our government from the self-serving career politicians, empire-building warmongers (neocons), and banksters. Please spread the word to help get the Monetary Revolution started. Thanks

#3) ' **The Impact of Fiat Money as the World's Reserve Currency'** ,   Aug-201

http://www.activistpost.com/2010/09/impact-of-fiat-money-as-worlds-reserve.html#more

http://www.infowars.com/the-impact-of-fiat-money-as-the-worlds-reserve-currency/

#4) 'A Plan to Save the Euro with Gold' ,   Nov-2011

http://www.activistpost.com/2011/11/three-step-plan-to-save-euro-with-gold.html#more

 http://blikskottel.wordpress.com/2012/01/28/redick-three-step-plan-to-save-the-euro/

http://www.pakalertpress.com/2011/12/02/a-three-step-plan-to-save-the-euro-with-gold/

#5) 'Convert the USA Monetary System to Gold',
Jan-2012

http://www.activistpost.com/2012/01/convert-usa-monetary-system-to-gold.html#more

#6) 'Germany Should Quit the Euro and Use Gold As Money', Sep-2012

http://www.activistpost.com/2012/09/germany-should-quit-euro-and-use-gold.html#more

http://www.qwmagazine.com/2012/09/03/germany-should-quit-the-euro-and-use-gold-as-money/

http://beforeitsnews.com/alternative/2012/09/germany-should-quit-the-euro-and-use-gold-as-money-2460646.html

#7) 'Will Basel III Allow Gold Money to Prevent a Crash of the USA Economy?', Nov-2012

http://www.activistpost.com/2012/11/will-basel-iii-allow-gold-money-to.html
http://beforeitsnews.com/alternative/2012/11/will-basel-iii-allow-gold-money-to-prevent-a-crash-of-the-usa-economy-2489634.html

#8) The U.S. Government and Consumers are Big Spenders Heading for a Crash , Jan-2015

http://www.activistpost.com/2015/01/the-us-government-and-consumers-are-big.html

Most U.S. citizens have been spoiled by the profits made from stock and real estate investments since 1990, and they see the 2008 crash as just a bump in the road. They are not aware that the hot economy was a bubble caused by excessive creation of new money (monetary inflation), and that a bigger crash is coming. The bubble started when Nixon cancelled the 1944 'Bretton Woods' gold standard agreement in 1971, which allowed the government to make money 'out of thin air'. Nixon cancelled because we had been creating billions of new USD to pay for the Vietnam War, LBJ's Medicare, etc. Other nations (especially our buddies England and France) were redeeming their 'falling value' paper dollars for gold because they knew we were running out! Since then our money supply has zoomed up, and the value of the US Dollar (USD) has fallen in purchasing power by over 90%. A good example is that a family car cost about $2,000 in the 1970s and is about $20,000 today. Most people think it is just price increases by greedy corporations, but in fact it is the lower purchasing power of the USD (which causes price inflation).

Even highly educated analysts make the same mistake. I was shocked to read the rosy evaluation of our economic condition, and future prospects, in a **Nov. 11, 2014 article by Jay Lehr Ph.D.**, Science Director of the Heartland Institute. He wrote; 'The U.S. economy is holding up well. Industrial production is at its highest point since 2008', then 'Jobless claims are at their lowest since 2000'. He uses a paragraph heading 'Bright U.S. Outlook'. He apparently believes that government management of the economy, such as the 'QE' series of money creation by the 'Federal Reserve System' (the 'Fed', our central bank), will create a rosy future. Switching gears, after a trip to Europe he said; 'They appear to be oblivious to their long-term problems.' Too bad he can't see (or won't say) the same in the U.S.!

For example, his article fails to mention;

1) Our massive (unpayable) government debt of $18 trn (admitted) and another about $130 trn (hidden) of unfunded liabilities for Medicare, pensions, etc. This is a big part of the reason that governments are promoting the lie that price inflation is a good thing, and deflation (lower prices because the money has higher purchasing power) is bad. They want to pay their debts with cheap money!!

2) The falling use of the USD as the world's primary reserve currency (was 80% of international transactions, now about 60%). Note that as the issuer of the world's primary reserve currency, we are the only nation that can create new money (via the Fed) to pay our bills! We have abused this (what French President Charles De Gaulle called our 'exorbitant privilege') by creating trillions of new dollars (monetary inflation), which will cause hyper price inflation (over 20% loss of value monthly) if we don't stop!

3) The inflation and jobless numbers are distorted by the government to keep them low,

4) The BRICS (Brazil, Russia, India, China, and S. Africa, plus more joining) are angry at U.S. imperial bully tactics and are avoiding the USD by dealing in their own currencies. To reduce dependency on the U.S. (and our bully tactics), they are creating a central bank, an IMF-style lender, and a funds processing (checks, deposits, etc.) network. The so-called 'Petrodollar' (Saudis have agreed to sell oil only for USD since 1974) is getting weaker as various producers sell in a variety of currencies and gold. Not selling oil for USD is a death sentence, and was a big part of why we invaded Iraq and Libya, and are poking Iran,

5) Our conversion to a consumer economy due to a massive amount of imports, funded by excessive amounts of new money (which only the issuer of the world's primary reserve currency can do), that results in 'offshoring' of jobs, factories, and technology.

This article is not meant to be a personal attack on Dr. Lehr. He is just a good example of an economist with Keynesian-Socialist-Progressive thinking, all of which tout a major role for government ownership and control of industry and the market. The 'Keynesian' brand of economics is named after British economist Lord John Maynard Keynes. In 1936 he published his **magnum opus "The General Theory of Employment, Interest and Money"**. The work served as a theoretical justification for the interventionist policies Keynes favored for ending a recession. Another example is Dr. Paul Krugman, an economist from Princeton University, who is the U.S. king of those who believe the government should 'manage' the economy, and ignore the bad results of the past. President Obama is another! In fact, he, and his successor, may use the next crash to convert the U.S. to a socialist government! They all explain failures by claiming the government 'didn't do enough!' Over 95% of economists (in colleges and think-tanks) follow this 'school of thought', with some Marxism (reduced property rights, more controls, etc.) included as deemed necessary. Their tenure, pensions, grants, and social life would drop if they disagreed with their Keynesian peers. I respect the 'Austrian' school of thought (started by Austrian economists) which emphasizes that there should be no market intervention (subsidies, price controls, etc.) by the government, and that entrepreneurs and sound money in a competitive free-market system will produce the most Peace, Prosperity and Liberty for all. History shows this to be correct, but politicians love to do favors for voters to get campaign contributions, which creates the 'crony capitalism' we have today. 'Austrian' type economists (Mises, Rothbard, Hoppe, etc.) have always had a hard time getting a teaching job.

Fake money is a key tool used by the 'Keynesian' economists and politicians. It pays for their wars and subsidies for 'friends', and grants, salaries, and pensions for themselves. Fake (or 'fiat') money is just paper with no value, but people are forced to use it by 'legal tender' laws which declare a 'face value'. Real (or 'sound') money is made of a commodity (gold and silver work best) which has market value even when not used as money. It acts as a medium of exchange, store of value, and unit of account for pricing (I prefer weight of gold; i.e. grams). In this case, gold has no 'price', just an exchange rate with other money. Example; What is the price of a US Dollar? Paper notes are OK as a convenience in handling, if redeemable for the commodity by any bearer on demand. Private mints should be allowed (no government monopoly). For details, see my essay **"A Plan to Convert the US Dollar to Gold as Money"**, and **my books on Amazon.com**. Dr. Lehr's 'Heartland Institute' showed their preference for big government when they lauded the June-2014 book *Money* by Steve Forbes and Elizabeth Ames. Its plan is 'big government' oriented by using the Fed to 'manage' the price of gold, and ignoring gold's 'store of value'. No free market here, but plenty of money for big government! Forbes has further credentials as a 'big government' conservative by his role as a Trustee for the 'big government, ultra-conservative' Heritage Foundation (Heritage.org), which gave 'war-monger, proud torturer' Dick Cheney one of their highest honors.

The truth is that the U.S. economic and social systems (subsidies, entitlements, etc.) are heading for another crash, and bigger than the one we had in 2008. We have all the characteristics of a failing empire; falling domestic production, big and increasing debt (government and personal), desperate politicians seeking more money and control (search for 'FATCA'), restricting rights of citizens, and endless wars to gain and retain powers. For details, see my essays, **"The Phases of an Empire"** and, **"The Cost of Building and Operating Empire (USA)."**

To avoid (or minimize) the next crash, we must; 1) End wars for empire (fight only for homeland defense), 2) Reduce government and personal debt, 3) Convert to gold as money, and 4) Comply with the Constitution.

This approach ALWAYS brings more Liberty, Peace, Justice, and Prosperity for ALL. Let's get started!

#9) **The Key Factors in a Sustainable Gold Standard for Money**, Aug-2014

http://www.activistpost.com/2014/08/the-key-factors-in-sustainable-gold.html#more

#10) **A Plan to Convert the US Dollar to Gold as Money,** Sep-2014

http://www.activistpost.com/2014/09/a-plan-to-convert-us-dollar-to-gold-as.html#more

#11) Benefits of a Gold-Money World

This is from p. 118 of Daves' book 'Monetary Revoulution USA'. We can expect the following benefits when the new gold money becomes legal:

1. More Peace: Wars are very expensive. The absence of an unlimited supply of fake money will inhibit the starting of wars; Diplomacy will be used instead. Imperialistic aggressors will have trouble getting funded.

2. More Prosperity: Gold money will increase in value (purchasing power) if percent economic growth exceeds the percent addition of newly mined gold. Savings will be rewarded, more money value will be available for investments, and managers can plan better.

3. Less Government: Governments need money to grow. Taxation has its limits, and in the absence of the unlimited supply of fake money, government programs, staffing, and spending will be limited. There will be less intervention in, and control of, our lives and work. More Liberty, Peace, and Prosperity will be the dividends.

4. Fewer and Smaller Business Cycles and Depressions:
The 'highs' of major business cycles are caused by bad investments due to excessive availability of money (credit and currency); too many new dollars chasing a limited number of deals, many of which are high risk. The incentive is to 'do something' with the excessive money. When the pool of money is reduced (Fed cutbacks) the frenzy drops like a rock. With a limited supply of real gold money, any frenzies would soon run out of money to feed them, and the cycles would be small or none.

5. Fewer Jobs 'Off-Shored': Due major increase in US wage and benefit costs after WW2, starting in the '80s, factories were built in other nations where costs are lower (first Mexico, then China, India, etc.) and the jobs moved out of the US! The same applies to software since the '90s. In addition, there is no limit to how much a country can import when it issues the world's reserve currency and can make it out of thin air. That's why our imports have soared since 1971 (when Nixon ended the dollar's tie to gold), and many of our factories have shut down. With gold as money, the importers run out of money, and local producers get the business. This is one of the self-regulating aspects of gold. (above '5.' was first published in Jan-2010)

6. Fewer Sovereign Defaults and No Currency Devaluations: In the past, many nations have defaulted (stopped payments) on some or all of their debt when they became overburdened, and then devalued (reduced face value) their currency to increase exports (lower prices). This robs lenders, and holders of the currency, but lets the nation enjoy a 'fresh-start', hopefully with reduced government spending and fewer anti-business laws. Argentina in 2002 is a recent example. When gold is money, the devalue option ends, which should give politicians and citizens incentive to keep their laws and economy more competitive. This new attitude will also reduce the excessive spending that leads to defaults. (above '6.' first published in Nov-2011).

We can enjoy these benefits, and avoid a crash of our economy, currency and lifestyle if we implement this plan for gold money. If we crash, meaning severe reduction in economic activity (depression), and 50% to 90% loss of purchasing power of the US dollar, we will need to rebuild from the 'ashes'. This can be viewed as an opportunity for the people to spontaneously start using gold as money. They will see its benefits, and demand to keep it! The laws can follow. Politicians will be desperate to keep their jobs so will cooperate to pass and repeal laws as needed; otherwise they will be fired and replaced.

It will require something like the above 'crash' circumstances, and a people-led Monetary Revolution, to take back our government from the self-serving career politicians, empire-building warmongers (neocons), and banksters.

Until the above changes are made, we need to defend ourselves against financial losses. **To see my ideas, look at chapter 5 'Investment Strategy' in my book** 'How to Protect and Grow Your Wealth'. **The book is available at amazon.com. Contact me at** RedickD@aol.com

#12) Standards for Gold-Based Monetary Systems:

From Daves' book; 'Monetary Revolution USA', p. 140

The gold standard is a **monetary system** in which the **unit of account (purchasing power)** is a weight of 24 ct **gold**.

1. The **Gold Specie Standard** is the system in which the monetary unit is associated with a circulating gold coin. (issuer claims to have 100% reserves for redemption of paper notes)

2. The **Gold Exchange Standard** may involve only the circulation of silver coins, or coins made of other metals, but the authorities will have guaranteed a fixed exchange rate with

another country that is on the gold standard, hence creating a *de facto* gold standard in that the value of the silver coins has a fixed external value in terms of gold that is independent of the intrinsic silver value. An example is the Bretton Woods Agreement of 1944.

3. The Gold Bullion Standard is a system in which gold coins do not actually circulate, but in which the authorities have agreed to sell gold bullion on demand at a fixed price.

(#16-1,2,3 from http://en.wikipedia.org/wiki/Gold_standard)

4. The **Private Gold Standard** version introduced here is based on 'Redick's Four Monetary Rules' (see #13, next below). Under this plan, money is produced by private firms in the free market where customers (users of money) decide which type and source of money they prefer, and mints compete for customers by supplying a good product. There is no central bank (our Fed), or legal tender laws, and government mints (run by the Treasury), if any, are optional, and have no control or privilege over the private mints. The free market is allowed to work! The 'unit of account', and thus prices, are **weight** of the commodity (typically gold and silver) used as money. Gold reserves (in physical possession of the mint) for redemption must be 100%, and must be published and audited.

#13) **'Redick's Four Monetary Rules'**, from Daves' book 'Monetary Revolution USA', p. 91. These rules describe the requirements for a monetary system using money made of a valuable commodity such as gold.

#14) **World Leaders Want to Replace the USD as the Worlds' Primary Reserve Currency'.**

http://www.activistpost.com/2016/10/elite-leaders-want-new-reserve-currency-crash-dollar.html, 7Oct16

1. Background on World Banking

There is always one currency that is treated as Primary because it is deemed safest (Issued by large, stable nation) and easy to use (available worldwide). This status is usually conferred by market usage, not a formal agreement (except Bretton Woods, 1944, below). Figure 1 shows the various currencies that have held Primary Reserve status.

Figure 1:

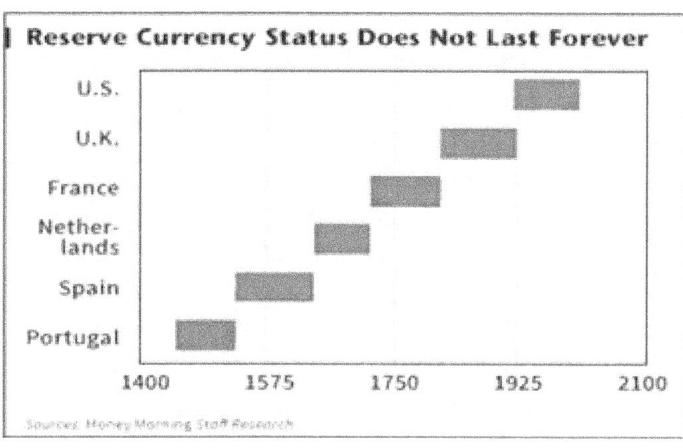

Notice that most keep reserve status for about 100 years and then, usually due to government 'tampering' with its' currency and economy, the nations' strength declines and their currency loses its' reserve status. Also notice that the USD has been 'reserve' since 1925, so has been in reserve status for 96 years. Watch out for decline! This fits with the fact that the USA is a failing empire, as discussed in this link to my article: http://www.activistpost.com/2013/09/empire-usa-is-crashing.html#more.

The development of the modern concept of a reserve currency took place in the mid nineteenth century (1850), with the introduction of national **central banks** worldwide and an increasingly **integrated global economy**." (more here; https://en.wikipedia.org/wiki/Reserve_currency)

After WW1, France and England were nearly broke due to war expenses and damage to factories and infrastructure. The USA emerged in 1918 as one of the world's strongest nations, with a strong currency based on our almost 6,000 tonnes of gold reserves, far ahead of the 1,201 held by France, and 1,046 by England. Thus, the U.S. Dollar became the worlds' Primary Reserve Currency.

After we spent too much during the Roaring 20s, we were getting low on gold for redeeming paper notes from Europe, etc. FDR got more gold (for free with paper Fed Notes, 'made out of thin air') by issuing Exec. Order 6102 in March, 1933, his first month in office. This Order made it illegal for U.S. citizens to own old (he called it 'hoarding') except for jewelry and rare coins. He paid citizens for their gold at the then official rate of $20.67 of paper Fed Notes per ounce (thus free to the government). (Note; The Gold Standard Act of 1900 set 1.5046 grams of pure 24k gold per dollar; thus $20.67 per troy ounce; 31.1 gr per troy oz./1.5046). He then repriced gold at $35 per ounce for a substantial profit. In 1974, Pres. Ford ended the prohibition to own gold.

The U.S. struggled with the Great Depression from 1932 until WW2 took over our economy from 1941 to 45. In 1944, when it had become clear that the USA and its' allies would win World War 2, financial leaders from all major countries agreed that they should meet to organize a plan on how international money and banking would be managed after the war. During July 1-22, 1944, 730 delegates from all 44 allied nations met at the Mount Washington resort in Bretton Woods, NH.

The meeting was called the 'United Nations Monetary and Financial Conference', but became known as the 'Bretton Woods Conference'. It established the rules for commercial and financial relations among the **United States** and all other signatory nations. The Bretton Woods system was the first example of a fully negotiated monetary order intended to govern monetary relations among independent nation-states. The chief features of the Bretton Woods system were an obligation for each country to adopt a **monetary policy** that maintained the **exchange rate** (± 1 percent) by tying its currency to gold and the ability of the **IMF** to bridge (bail out) temporary **imbalances of payments**. Also, there was a need to address the lack of cooperation among other countries and to prevent **competitive devaluation** of the currencies as well.

The delegates signed the Bretton Woods agreement on July 22, 1944. Setting up a system of rules, institutions, and procedures to regulate the **international monetary system**, these accords established the;

1. **International Monetary Fund** (IMF) and 2. The 'International Bank for Reconstruction and Development' (IBRD), which today is part of the 3. **World Bank Group**.

These are the first world-wide banking organizations. A banking network called SWIFT (Society for Worldwide Interbank Financial Telecommunications), was built in 1973 by the U.S. who still operates and controls it. Member banks use it to send and receive information about financial transactions in a secure, standardized and reliable environment. It supplies information, but does not execute transactions. **This network, and the status as Reserve Currency, gives the USA power to abuse other nations for both economic and political issues. This disturbs/angers the other members and since the late 1960s (after abuse since 1944) they have wanted to unseat the U.S. from this perch.**

The United States, which controlled two thirds of the world's gold in 1944 (US=20,279 tonnes), insisted that the Bretton Woods system rest on both gold and the USD. The USD was voted to immediately be the worlds' primary reserve currency, and this made the USD 'good as gold', (By law for the first time; normally it is earned by usage.). All banks were now required to hold it in their reserves. This is needed because it was used in over 70% of international transactions, even when the U.S. was not a party to the transaction). This is more convenient than keeping a supply of over 100 currencies, but gives power to the issuer of the Primary Reserve.

The agreement required that the U.S. redeem Fed Notes (gold for paper money) to any nation on demand. By the early 1960s, other nations knew that **we had been paying most of our bills** (with large expenses for Medicare, welfare, and Vietnam) **by creating new money** (paper or digital) **'out of thin air'** and soon would not have enough gold to redeem all of the issued notes and bonds. Only the issuer of the worlds' primary reserve currency can get away with this! French President DeGaulle called it our 'exorbitant privilege'. Germany, France and England held millions of EuroDollars from U.S. spending on the Marshal Plan and exports to the U.S., and felt at risk of a default on redemption, so they began redeeming much of their USD holdings for gold during the late 1960s. By 1970 U.S. gold reserves were approaching zero and President Nixon met with his financial advisors to make a plan to avoid depletion. Thus, on 15 August 1971, the United States unilaterally terminated **convertibility** of the USD to **gold**, effectively bringing the Bretton Woods system to an end, and rendering the dollar a **fiat currency**. (worth whatever the issuing government declares as its' 'face value'). This action, referred to as the '**Nixon shock**', created the situation in which the U.S. dollar became the worlds' first fiat **reserve currency** (rather than gold), and was accepted still by nations and sellers. With a year, all world currencies became free-floating (fiat, not redeemable for a commodity) and were valued (exchange rate with USD) in free markets (not by law). Since 1971 the U.S. has been abusive in creating new money to pay most of its' bills, and thus the **purchasing power (PP) per USD** has declined. Econ 101 says if you increase the quantity of an item, and demand stays flat, its value per unit will decline; ie, monetary inflation causes depreciation of purchasing power. Due to monetary inflation (excessive creation of new money) the USD has lost over 95% of its' value (PP) since creation of the Fed in 1913. The rate of decline was fastest after Nixon ended redemption for gold in 1971. Recent examples are that a room in Motel 6 cost $6 in the 70s and is $50 now, and a family car that cost $2,000 in the 70s is now over $20,000! This shows that the purchasing power of the USD has declined by about 90% since the 1970s, and means $1,000 in 1976 was worth $100 in 2016; an average loss of 2.25% per year! This loss should be included in any investment analysis (annuities, CDs, etc.).

2. Monetary Events Since 2000

We again see that our trading partner nations and firms (who hold many dollars received for exports to the U.S.) feel at risk as the USD declines. Here is activity from the major players.

At the IMF, the BANCOR: The IMF recommended on April 13, 2010 that the world adopt **a global fiat currency called the "Bancor"**, and that a **global central bank** be established to administer it. That is 'big talk', so let's watch it closely.

In the USA: The Fed has been desperately trying to 'manage' our money and economy since the 2007 bust. The massive injection of new money by the 'Quantitative Easing' method (Fed buys bonds from banks), active from 2008 to 2014, with QE1, 2, and 3. It failed to stimulate the economy despite increasing Fed assets from $700 billion to $4.5 trillion, for an insertion of $3.8 trillion into the U.S. banking industry! The low interest rates since then did not spurred borrowing or spending, because people and firms sought safety in less of both. However the low rates help the government by reducing interest payments on our massive $20 trillion national debt (plus $146 trillion more of undisclosed debts). Thus, we stumble along toward the debt default cliff.

In Mar-2016 a bill was introduced in the U.S. Senate called the **'DIGIT Act' (Developing Innovation and Growing the Internet of Things Act).** This bill requires the Department of Commerce to convene a working group of stakeholders to provide recommendations to Congress on how to plan for and encourage the proliferation of the Internet of Things (IoT) in the United States. Some say it will support digital money.

China, Russia, and the BRICS: China and Russia suggested at the Jan-2009 'World Economic Forum' in Davos that a new system is needed to replace the USD as the world's primary reserve currency **(Think: We need a single world currency!!)**, then they agreed to start trading in their own currencies (the USD declined due to less demand). In Aug-2011, China and France agreed to form a task force to discuss how the Yuan could become part of the SDR (SDR= Special Drawing Rights). The SDR is an asset (not currency) made of a 'basket of currencies', used only between member central banks of the IMF). In Dec-2011 China and Japan agreed to trade in their own currencies. In Jan-2012 Iran said it would sell oil to India in Rupees. China holds $1.3 trillions of USD denominated bonds and other assets, and doesn't want the USD to crash (but they do want a controlled decline).

In late 2015 the IMF announced it would make the Chinese Renminbi currency part of the SDR, and they did! **On Oct 20, 2016, the IMF announced that the Yuan is now part of the SDR,** which will likely send billions of dollars moving around the world, literally overnight! **Some say this could cause a serious reduction in the exchange value of the USD!**

The BRICS: A group called the BRICS (Brazil, Russia, India, China, and S. Africa) started trading with each other in their own currencies in 2011. They hold annual conferences. At the July-2014 sixth summit of the BRICS in Brazil they started funding of **two multilateral financial institutions** designed to erode the dominance of the World Bank and International Monetary Fund as arbiters of the global economic system. Namely: 1) A $100 billion **New Development Bank'** (like the World Bank), and 2) a Reserve Currency Fund (like the IMF) worth another $100 billion.

Russia: Vladimir Putin, at the 11th meeting of the **Valdai International Discussion Club** in Sochi, on Oct.24, 2014, said, *" Russia is making strides in assembling a massive new trading bloc known as the **Eurasian Union**. When it opened for business on January 1, 2015, Russia, Belarus, and Kazakhstan became a barrier-free market with 170 million people and a GDP of $2.7 trillion.."* The Union will further reduce demand for the USD, and thus reduce its' value (purchasing power).

China: China made a major announcement on Oct. 24, 2014 with the creation the **Asian Infrastructure Investment Bank (AiiBank.org)**, a **multilateral development bank** to provide finance to infrastructure projects in the **Asia** region. AIIB is regarded by some as a rival for the **IMF**, the **World Bank** and the **Asian Development Bank** (ADB), which are dominated by developed countries like the United States. As of April 15, 2015, almost all Asian countries and most major countries outside Asia (total of 50) had joined the AIIB, except the US, Japan (which dominated the ADB) and Canada. North Korea's and Taiwan's applications for Prospective Founding Member (PFM) were rejected. The rush of our 'friends' in Europe to join is an indication of China's growing economic power. It is not clear which currency the AIIB will use. It could be the Yuan, or even the IMF SDR, with the Yuan included. Either choice would reduce the USD dominance as a reserve currency, an ominous step toward collapse of the US economy!! On Aug. 4, 2015 the IMF announced the above SDR changes would **NOT** occur at the IMF annual meeting to be held in Lima, Peru in Oct-2015! This rejection was pushed by the U.S. based on the fact that China's debt is 280% of their GDP, thus too weak to be part of the SDR. Then on Nov. 13, 2015, IMF chief Christine Lagarde said the fund now deemed the yuan "meets the requirements to be a 'freely usable' currency" -- a key hurdle to joining the yen, dollar, pound, and euro as a leading unit in international trade. This implied the yuan (same as 'Renminbi'-RMB- when used as an external currency) could be formally admitted to the IMF's "special drawing rights" currency basket at the IMFs' Nov. 30, 2015 meeting in Sweden. Indeed, at the meeting the IMF announced their approval of the Chinese renminbi as one of the world's main central bank reserve currencies, and part of the SDR.

As shown in Table 1 below, minor changes in the percent of each currency in the SDR left the USA almost the same. The changes took effect on Oct. 1, 2016.

Table 1:	**Percent of SDR Value**				
	US$	Euro	Yen	Pound	Renminbi
ISO Code:	USD	EUR	JPY	GBP	CNY or RMB
Now	41.9	37.4	9.4	11.3	0.0
New	41.73	30.93	8.33	8.09	10.92
Change	-0.17	-6.47	-1.07	-3.2	+ 10.92

Many financial people expected a sharp market reaction such as reduction of the USD value (USDX.com, Bloomberg.com) now that it had more competition, plus an uptick in gold (due to the weaker USD), but gold actually dropped $60 per oz. (4.9%) from Sep.30 to Oct. 5, 2016. I attribute the gold decline to buyers knowing about the Oct. 1 change a year in advance, so the market effect had already occurred.

The IMF decision will help pave the way for broader use of the renminbi in trade and finance, securing China's standing as a global economic power. Chinese leaders view it as a giant step up for their place in world economics! The trouble is that much of the increase in demand for the yuan/renminbi will reduce demand for the USD, and its' purchasing power will fall even faster.

Peter Schiff (SchiffGold.com) said; '"*Another issue is a possible Chinese move to un-peg the yuan from the dollar, which **could set off an earthquake. When the Chinese decide to abandon their peg both for the Hong Kong dollar and the yuan – that is going to be a 10.0 on the Richter scale of economic activity. That is going to be huge. This time, it's going to be the dollar that takes it on the chin.**"*
We will soon see!

To gain even more credibility, China may announce their current holdings of gold, which have been secret since revealed as 1,054 tonnes in 2009. They probably have over 5,000 tonnes now, which would make them a close second to the 8,134 tonnes the US 'claims' to have (probably much less due to sales and hypothecation –using as collateral for loans-)! The changes China made in Aug-2015 to devalue the yuan (to increase exports), have added to the complexity!
Read more at: **http://www.pinnacledigest.com/articles/world-currency-born**

All of the above changes are aimed at ending the USD Status as the Worlds' Primary Reserve Currency, weakening the USD, and the associated control the USA has on world banking and politics.

The Eurozone: Nations that use the Euro currency have their own set of problems related to decline of the Euro and the increase of intervention in their sovereign affairs by the EU and its' bank. The huge Deutschebank is in big trouble, including trillions of derivatives. For more, search for articles about 'EU,exit' and 'Brexit'.

The above discussion shows there is much support for replacing the USD reserve status with 'something'.

3. **Conclusion: How the BRICS Plan to Replace the USD as the Worlds' Primary Reserve Currency**

During the last 40 years, there has been much discussion worldwide about how a new world currency (a new SDR?) could be 'substituted' for all of the different currencies that exist today. This would end U.S. dominance by giving power to the group (the IMF?) that manages it. In a perverse way, this could be a means for the U.S. to 'substitute' its' unpayable $20 Trillion debt into the 'New SDR', and thus avoid losses for holders of bonds now denominated in USD! The word 'substitution' is used when a new currency replaces, or redeems, another.

Please excuse the need to type the two links below into your PC, but space does not allow a full printing of the text.

a) The link below, from Feb-2011, plus a printed excerpt from the first few pages, gives background on how the 'substitution' concept got started, and how long its' supporters have been pushing for it.
http://money.cnn.com/2011/02/10/markets/dollar/index.htm
Title; IMF Calls for Dollar Alternative
By Ben Rooney, staff reporter February 10, 2011

b) The article in the link below was written by Willem Middelkoop in Aug-2016 (CDFund.com). He is the author of 'The Big Reset', first published in 2013. In 2007 his first book was published in the Netherlands, titled 'Als de dollar valt' (When the Dollar Falls). He surveys how 'substitution' has been discussed for over 40 years, and is getting more active. A few pages are shown below.

Title: IMF's 'Substitution Fund' to kick-start SDR as New Global Currency?

http://www.cdfund.com/wp-content/uploads/2016/08/SDR-Special-aug2016-DEF.pdf

The Chinese, ever more in the driving seat of global finance, have made it very clear that the Special Drawing Rights (SDR or IMF-money) of the IMF is the preferred future international world reserve currency. A great example of China's frustration over U.S. monetary policies can be found in comments distributed by the Chinese official state press agency Xinhua a few years ago; 'Politicians in Washington have done nothing substantial but postponing once again the final bankruptcy of global confidence in the U.S. financial system'.

****

Daves' Closing Comments: Thank you for your interest in learning about this very important topic. In the next few years, I believe we will see action on the ideas mentioned in this article (or radical new ones!). All persons and firms should be diligent to avoid, or at least minimize, any bad effects of the changes could have on their investments. Precious metals will have a prominent role. For now, visit Chapter 4 in my book 'How to Protect and Grow Your Wealth'.. Please send your questions or comments to me at RedickD@aol.com.

Thanks and Good Luck.

#15) Table 1: Weight Measures: Common units for precious metals are:

1 Tonne (metric) = 2,205 pounds (Lbs) = 1,000 Kilograms (Kg)
                = 32,150 troy oz.
1 US Ton (Short) = 2,000 Lbs advp.   =   907.2 Kg
1 UK Ton (Long) = 2,240 Lbs advp.   = 1,016.5 Kg
1 gram   = 15.43 grains = 5 metric carats = 0.643 pennyweight
1 Troy Ounce = 31.10 grams = 480 grains (gr)= 120 engl. carats
1 Troy Pound   = 12 Troy ounces (Oz) = 373.2 grams
1 Avoirdupois Lb= 16 avp. ounces= 453.6 grams=7,000 grains
1 Avp. ounce   = 28.35 grams (g), 437.5 grains
1 English carat   = 1.296 metric carats (for precious stones)

% Gold	Europe System Fineness	Carat System
100.0	1.000	24 carat
91.7	0.917	22
75.0	0.750	18
58.5	0.585	14
41.6	0.416	10

Notes for Table 1:
1. The 'Long Ton' is the Imperial system used in the UK
2. The 'Short Ton' is used in the US and Canada.
3. The IMF and all nations measure their gold in metric tonnes.
4. Gold weighs 19,320 kg per cubic meter. Tungsten is close at 19,600, so it is sometimes gold plated and used as fake gold bars and ingots. Steel is 7,850, copper 8,930, lead 11,340,and water 1,000.
5. Grains, grams, and Tonne are metric units. The Troysystem was started by King Henry II of England. The Avoirdupois system evolved through common usage in Europe.
6. Fineness: The purity of a precious metal measured in 1,000 parts of an alloy: a gold bar of 0.995 fineness contains 995 parts gold and 5 parts of another metal; a 0.999 coin is 99.9% pure.
7. A sample calculation from p. 82: The Gold Standard Act of 1900 set 1.5046 grams of pure 24k gold per dollar; thus $20.67 per troy ounce; 31.1 gr per troy oz./1.5046.

Blank

Blank

C. Text of articles about 'General Economic and Social Issues'

Article Contents: (# followed by a 'T' means the text is shown)

Page   Title

****

#1) A Vision for State-Owned Banking in Wisconsin'
Aug-2010

http://www.activistpost.com/2010/08/vision-for-state-owned-banking-in.html

#2) ' How is Independent Thinking Connected to Freedom and Prosperity ', Aug-2010

 http://www.activistpost.com/2010/08/how-is-independent-thinking-connected.html

Independent thinking is the basis for understanding the world around us. This means that you only believe and support information and ideas that make sense to you, after proper analysis, based on facts and logic. That is the opposite of accepting whatever the masses, your church, political party, or

the government says is "right" or "true." For those
people, Lemming, sheep, follower, and herd mentality come to
mind.

Independent thinking means that you are rational and take
responsibility for your life and thoughts, rather than seeking
emotional security, or righteousness, by being a "normal"
submissive dupe, or "believer" in whatever is most accepted
around you. It means no-fair labeling those who are
Independent Thinkers as "conspiracy theorists," "kooks," or
"radicals," just because they disagree with mainstream
thought. Especially if they: A) Base their opinions on fact and
logic. B) Are non-violent. C) Their goals tend to restore
liberty, honesty, rule of law, and the Constitution to our nation.

Don't think this only applies to the ill-informed masses. Many
educated and successful people also reside in the security
and convenience of the willing-dupe pit; in fact, many are
active parasites who seek government money or special laws
for personal gain. Most are affected by being careful to not
endanger their pension, promotion, a grant, social acceptance,
etc. Hence, our national decline of ethics, peace, and
prosperity.

Most people don't care much beyond their current wants and
needs, but they should; it is the future, and a broader view of
national affairs that they should be concerned about — if only
for their children and future generations. Key future issues
(some in 1 to 5 years) are: A) Costly and deadly wars for
Empire (not defense). B) Corruption in
government. C) Reduced living standards caused **by crash**
of the US Dollar.

Successful leaders make strong use of Independent Thinking,
hopefully mixed with an ample supply of ethics. We need more
of them. H.L. Mencken said it well:

"The most dangerous man, to any government, is the man
who is able to think things out for himself without regard to the
prevailing superstitions and taboos. Almost inevitable he

comes to the conclusion that the government he lives under is dishonest, insane and intolerable, and so, if he is romantic, he tries to change it. And even if he is not romantic personally he is apt to spread discontent among those who are."

#3) 'Excessive Spending, Taxation, and Controls are Destroying the U.S. Economy' , Jan-2011

http://www.activistpost.com/2011/01/how-excess-spending-taxation-and.html

Politicians, 'Progressive' activists, NeoCon Imperialists, and bankers worldwide love to spend money and love the unending supply of it from; 1. taxing 'other people,' and 2. fiat paper money ('face value' decreed by government) from the central banks that create and control it. With this supply, the politicians never run out of money for their vote-for-me pork; Progressive activists get it for their welfare and subsidy projects; Imperialists for their wars and 'foreign aid' bribery; and bankers get cash and credit for the reserves they need to continue lending and for creating bizarre investment schemes. All four view the government and its central bank (ours is the Federal Reserve System, or 'Fed') as the unlimited source of funding to finance their projects, and bail them out if they get into trouble.

Of course, most of these handouts come with strings attached, so the federal government gains creeping power over state and personal matters. The controls that should be removed are those that limit choices by consumers, or do favors for political friends. Many controls start as a means to protect citizens from violation of their rights by others, which is a proper function of government. The problems start when controls are enacted to limit people, even when what they do is no harm or threat to others. This is the 'nanny' approach, where government manages our lives.

One part of the solution is to make licenses optional for the professions such as medical, law, etc., and trades such as plumbers, hairdressers, etc. Users would be able to choose 'licensed' or 'independent' based on price and track-record (references) of the product or service provider. This would introduce competition to the license-cartels that now control pricing and limit addition of new members. Prices would drop and service quality and availability would improve.

The 'Building codes' and 'zoning laws' now written and enforced by counties often impose excessive costs (minimum size of house, special plumbing, wiring, and insulation requirements, etc.) that decrease availability of 'affordable housing.' Adherence to these codes should also be optional for private buildings (houses, garages, barns) where the user-occupants make the choices, but would apply to 'public' buildings like apartments, stores, offices, factories where occupants are not part of the construction choices or ownership.

Zoning laws are usually created to separate residential and commercial areas, but cover broad areas which ignore or conflict with local preferences. The laws are often abused by including excess restrictions such as approved 'colors' or 'architectural style' for houses, etc. These laws should be replaced by voluntary neighborhood associations, which are a means of self-defense. There are many other types of excess controls, but these will be addressed in a future essay.

Further, this loose, cheap money creates the moral hazard of false confidence that causes businessmen, politicians, and bankers to engage in expensive and risky deals (new factories, wars for oil and bases, welfare, derivatives, no-doc home mortgages, etc.) that they would otherwise avoid, or could not finance. More and bigger wars, spending, and business cycles (bubbles) are the result.

Big spending got a boost in 1913 when the Fed was created (fake money funded two World Wars, VietNam, Medicare, etc.), and another major jump occurred when Nixon cut the dollar's last ties to gold in 1971; we were running out and we had no limits on the amount of fake money we could create. Being the world's reserve currency allowed us to do this, since our dollar — even those newly created — were treated as 'good as gold.' Due to this added increase in excess spending and borrowing since 1971, the US has declined from the world's biggest lender to the biggest borrower, and our growing national debt of $14 trillion is now about equal to our Gross National Product, which all economists agree is dangerous. Our problems are very similar to those that caused the recent crashes in Greece and Ireland, and which have Spain, Portugal and England on the brink. How did we get into this mess? Why do people seek *more* government when history is so full of economic and human loss due to central control of the economy?

The Start of Our Decline
The USA started a trend toward more government in 1933 when FDR announced the New Deal. The Great Depression was caused by excess 'stimulus' money created by the Fed in the 1920s that led to mal-investments and bubbles that burst in 1929 (they always do). In a similar manner, today's TARP and Quantitative Easing schemes are flooding our economy with money, with little benefit and much harm.

FDR tried to end the depression with government spending by his New Deal. This postured the government for the first time in US history in a paternalistic (nanny) way as funder and manager of the economy, and much of our personal lives. This Paternalism violates the Constitution, which mainly empowers the government to protect our rights, and is the opposite of the personal responsibility and initiative that built our country, thus marking the beginning of our decline.

The New Deal funded the 'Progressive-Liberal-Socialistic' (pick a term; they all seek free benefits from big government) projects that continue in various forms today, and are the main cause of our excess, and unsustainable, spending and borrowing at both the State and Federal level. I include in this group the former Liberals who became 'neo-conservatives' to push their imperial agenda (they and Pres. Obama ended the Liberal anti-war movement) with the false Conservatives such as Presidents R. Nixon and G. W. Bush. This imperial thinking has led to our chosen role as the World's Policeman (or bully?) since 1945, and the huge costs of our 'defense' equipment, military people, contractors, and bases (about 1,000 in 130 countries), which exceeds the total spending of all other nations combined!

This can be called **Empire-USA**, and must end. The nations we 'protect' with our SOFAs (Status of Forces Agreements), save billions of dollars of 'defense' expense by trading some control of their skies, land and economy for our presence. Maybe we should declare the USA as a neutral country like Sweden or Switzerland? As a 'neutral' we would only need homeland defense (low cost, similar to Sweden and Switzerland), and would have additional reasons to eliminate the Patriot Act, FISA, TSA, MCA, etc., when the blowback from our overseas invasions, killings, tortures, and meddling ends.

As opposed to false conservatives such as Nixon and both Bushes, a true Conservative or Libertarian is for low spending and taxes, sound money, adherence to the Constitution (limited government), social freedom, and a non-interventionist foreign policy. Thus, under true Conservative-Libertarian leadership: a) our Federal spending would be reduced by more than half, and b) The unlimited supply of fake money would end by abolishing the Fed. Money would be limited in quantity, and made of, or backed-by, precious metal (silver and/or gold), the unit of account (price of things) would be by weight of the metal — grams, not dollars, dimes, etc. — with private mints and no central bank or legal-tender laws.

Of course most economists are now in the Liberal (more-government; Keynesian style) camp, especially the grant-seeking academics. As a result of this Progressive dominance during most of the years since 1933, our nation, the US Dollar, and many states are now facing economic collapse.

History is full of the failure of nations and empires. Most fail due to excess government control, high costs, and corruption, plus a decline of personal responsibility in the people due to the moral hazards of laziness and excess consumption caused by subsidized or free goods and services. The USA is on the brink.

Success Stories for Limited Government

Conversely, in the last fifty years we have seen the recovery of countries that suffered economic failure (low Liberty, GDP, and standard of living) due to excess government control, when they introduced some free-market capitalism as a means to end their decline. Examples are:

1. USSR: In 1985 General Secretary Mikhail Gorbachev introduced Glasnost (openness of government activity) and Peristroika (restructuring, privatization) at the same time. It didn't work because: a) the Russian people had lost their desire and skills to take initiative, and b) the corrupt Apparatchiks (former Communists bureaucrats) and Oligarchs (business magnates) grabbed ownership of the industries that were divested, often at fraudulently low prices. The USSR is gone, and surviving Russia still has serious problems with corruption and low productivity, but at least its homeland still exists and is trying to reform.

2. Vietnam: Since we stopped bombing and murdering them in 1975, Vietnam has made a shift from a highly-centralized planned economy to a socialist-oriented market economy which uses limited central control, and much free-enterprise by the people. It is working well, but Liberty remains low.

3. Most of the former Soviet-controlled countries in eastern Europe (Eastern Bloc) have reduced central planning, and increased free-enterprise in various amounts, and the results are good to the extent government control has been reduced. Poland and the Czech Republic have done best because of their leaders and a spirit of initiative in the people. Even Cuba

has tried some free-enterprise in a desperate move to avoid collapse.

4. India is a good example of choosing to reform due to the failure of central planning, and prohibition of foreign investment. Following the socialist inspired economy after its 1947 independence from Britain, in 1990 India allowed international competition and foreign investment. Results have been excellent, but a high percent of the population are still poor. Economists predict that by 2020, India will be among the leading economies of the world.

5. China: We have seen the People's Republic of China rise as an economic success after they allowed free-enterprise to create new products, services, and exports. Since the revolution in 1949, the political campaigns led by Mao Zedong, such as the Great Leap Forward and the Cultural Revolution, are blamed for 40 to 70 millions of deaths, causing severe famine and damage to the culture, society and economy of China. After Mao's death in 1976, his main leftist supporters, led by the Gang of Four, were ousted in a coup, and reformists led by Deng Xiaoping took power in 1978, and started economic reforms based on more free-enterprise, but with considerable central government ownership and control. Civil liberties have remained low, but 'Free Trade Zones' have grown to larger areas. The economic reforms occurred in two stages. The first stage, staring in 1978, involved the decollectivization of agriculture, the opening up of the country to foreign investment, and permission for entrepreneurs to start-up businesses. However, most industry remained state-owned, inefficient and acted as a drag on economic growth. The second stage of reform, in the late 1980s and 1990s, involved the privatization and contracting out of much state-owned industry and the lifting of price controls, protectionist policies, and regulations, although state monopolies in sectors such as banking and petroleum remained. The private sector grew remarkably, accounting for as much as 70 percent of China's GDP by 2005, a figure larger in comparison to many Western nations. From 1978 to 2010, unprecedented growth

occurred, with the economy increasing by 9.5% a year, and China's economy became the second largest after the United States, and also the world's largest holder of US debt at about $900 billion (or over $1 trillion when Hong Kong's holdings are included). The conservative Hu-Wen Administration more heavily regulated and controlled the economy after 2005, reversing some reformist gains. For 2010, China was ranked 140th among 179th countries in Heritage Foundation's Index of Economic Freedom World Rankings, which is an improvement from the preceding year.

Conclusion
Again, why do some Americans seek more government when history is so full of economic and human loss due to central control of the economy? They will cite the success of some of the above hybrid socialist-oriented market economies (but not all attempts are a big success, depending on leaders and rules, but free markets always bring some improvement), as to why they want it for the USA, but that would include giving-up most of our Liberty, and the present hybrid system is failing all around us! I say these people want more government because: a) they are delusional 'do-gooders' who are ignorant of, or ignore, the past (or think 'we'll do it right this time'), and are determined to impose their views of 'common good' and 'shared responsibility' on others by force of law. They all focus on the good parts, and ignore the bad side-effects. (I suggest private charity), b) they see a benefit in it for themselves (free health care, tuition, tenure, etc.), and/or c) they seek the prestige, power, security, and wealth that comes with being in charge of government programs (even when they know there is much harm being done; employees of the Fed are classic). Shame on all three types!

The problems with the Progressive system are: 1. It is immoral due to using 'tyranny of the majority' gang-theft to impose a higher tax rate on certain groups ('the rich', inheritors, property owners, corporations, etc.), and they want more even though the top 20% of earners already pay about 80% of our tax revenue. They justify these tax attacks by claiming 'the rich' are lucky, more fortunate, etc., while ignoring the fact that most high net-worth people earned their wealth by work, risk, investment, and brains; 2. It damages personal responsibility, social values, and private charity while creating a fragile entitlement-based dependency for both people and business (nurturing ties with friends and family means less when you perceive 'the government' as your best friend); and 3. It creates an unfriendly national and state regime of taxes and fees that scare away successful people and firms, and thus causes a net loss in tax revenues. Individuals and firms are moving to other countries. WI, IL, CA and other high-tax-and-spend states are losing people and businesses to low-tax-and-spend states like TX and FL. Texas gained four new Congressional seats in the last census!

The economic and social problems we face today are clear notice that the day of reckoning has arrived. Taxes, regulations, spending, paternalism, and our empire of bases and meddling worldwide must be reduced, or our economy and social order will collapse, as it has for all previous empires (UK, Spain, USSR, France, etc.) that failed to heed the warnings!

4) Free-Market Choices Can Solve Our Health Care Problems' , March-2011

http://www.activistpost.com/2011/03/how-free-market-choices-can-solve-our.html

(Also read Issue #8 on p. 159)

Until the 1930s, the US health care system was customer-based, where each person decided which services to use and paid for them directly. The needy were often given discounts by the doctors and hospitals. Abuse was minimal because people knew each other and valued their reputations. This has evolved to the mix of employer, government, and insurance-controlled plans we have today.

Abuse is rampant (excess services and fraudulent billings) because most people don't mind cheating the government. A major step occurred in the 1930s when hospitals organized Blue Cross, and doctors created Blue Shield, to guarantee themselves a steady income stream by having patients — and later, their employers — prepay for medical care on a subscription basis. Wage controls during WW2 led to employers offering 'group' health and life insurance as an 'extra' to attract scarce workers. After the war, these benefits were perceived as a 'normal' part of any good job. People with 'existing conditions' (the 'pre' is redundant) were absorbed into the group plans with little impact. As part of his 'Great Society' program, Pres. L. Johnson created Medicare (Parts A, B, and C; for seniors), and Medicaid (for the needy; paid 50 to 83% by the Federal government, but operated by the states) in 1965. Drugs were added to Medicare as Part D in 2006.

Today we are in the midst of massive federal government intervention in our health care system because Congress passed the 'Patient Protection and Affordable Care Act' (PPACA; 'Obamacare') which became law on March 23, 2010. The law claims to reform the private health insurance market by; 1. providing better coverage for those with existing conditions, 2. improving prescription drug coverage in Medicare, and 3. extending the life of the Medicare Trust fund by at least 12 years. Sounds nice! However, it's clearly unconstitutional (no authority in the Constitution, forced purchase of insurance, etc.), and this is just a start. Instead of a 'single payer' system run by the government (like Canada, France, Mexico, etc.), it dumps the costs on; 1. the insurance industry, which then must boost its rates and rules to handle the increased benefits, and 2. the states with increased Medicaid users.

Choice is being replaced by coercion!

Government Plans

In any country with 'national single-payer' care (doctors are government employees, all citizens must belong, etc.), government budgets are a huge issue as to which services and medicines are available, and to whom (rationing). The medical specialists and equipment for expensive services such as organ transplants are limited, and people wait for years and sometimes die. In some national programs, the death rates from breast and prostate cancer are twice to three times higher than in the United States. You can't see a specialist (ear, eye, skin, etc.) without referral by a family doctor. Old people are sometimes deemed 'not worth it' for expensive treatments and drugs.

It was illegal in Canada to open a private 'for fee' clinic, since it was deemed unfair to those who can't afford it, but that is changing. Canadian health managers now admit that their system is financially 'unsustainable' (same in England, France and others), and that formerly illegal 'private services' (non-government doctors who charge a fee) and private insurance will be needed to avoid collapse. Some provinces already allow certain private services, and even pay private hospitals to take care of 'public' patients. Government doctors even suggest use of private care to avoid the delays, and to off-load patients. From my personal experience living in Canada, I found doctors to be less courteous, since to them patients are not valued clients, but just more work. At the extreme (Russia, etc.), corruption sets in, and doctors and staff demand bribes for access to services.

In countries with a long history of rule by monarchs, or socialism, I find that government is viewed as a combination of Boss and Mother, and the people are submissive to the rules and treatment. Those who don't like it, leave. The USA was founded in a spirit of Liberty, and some people still prize it, but since the 1930s when FDR declared the government owed you 'a good life', the majority of people now seek benefits paid by 'someone else' ('the rich', property owners, inheritors, etc.). The growth of government spending and debt in the last seventy years (especially since 1971 when Nixon took us off the gold standard) has grown to such extremes (debt now equals the GDP!) that we face a crash in the economy and value of the dollar. Funding will drop or end for most government programs. The sudden onset will prevent seeking alternatives in time, and many people will suffer or die.

In the free-market plan below, I show how medical costs can be reduced, even while increasing quality. It is based on less government spending and control, and more personal responsibility. Private charity will blossom as the people take charge. This produces a moral and sustainable program of good health for all. It sets goals that will take time to achieve, but if we start the step-by-step transition now, the results will soon show and the goals will be achieved.

Dave's Free-Market Plan
This plan is aimed at getting the government out of patient-doctor-hospital control and funding so that positive free-market incentives guide the patients and doctors: This will reduce cost, improve care, and preserve our civil rights and liberty. The items below all start in parallel on a planned-transition basis. Existing care will be maintained as the changes take place.

1) Repeal Obamacare, phase-out Medicare and Medicaid, and allow states to create their own plans for seniors and the needy. Care for war veterans would continue without change. As a transition, the Federal government would issue quarterly vouchers to all former Medicare and Medicaid recipients until their state system is in service. The vouchers would be useable only for paying health expenses and insurance, and be the same amount for everyone. This would let people shop for the privately provided services they need. Special vouchers would be issued to those with major 'existing conditions' that preclude their purchasing insurance, with payments continuing until the end of their illness, or until death. The value of any voucher would be owned by each person, and could be transferred; a) to their account in another state if they move, b) as a gift, or by a will upon death, to other qualified people. Vouchers are a form of Health Savings Account (HSA, see item 10), and give incentive to avoid unhealthy life styles (obesity, excess alcohol, etc.) and non-essential visits to, and treatments and tests by, the doctor.

2) Reduce costs by greater use of Physician Assistants (PAs) so a doctor's time is not wasted on routine work the assistant can perform (including clinics run by PAs; see Item 9 below).

3) Use the FDA only to determine and disclose possible side-effects and viability of drugs, but not restrict use of them (or their potency) until there are virtually no side-effects: Let doctor judgment and CONSUMER CHOICE rule! At present, the FDA people withhold use of drugs too long, so they won't be criticized, while people die.

4) Bring the lower price and higher quality benefits
of competition, and consumer choice into health care by
busting the medical pricing cartel and allowing doctors to
advertise their rates (web sites, newspaper ads, etc.), training
and results records. The American Medical Association
(AMA), and professional societies, now 'discourage' or prevent
this. Allow doctors to practice as members of private, non-
government sanctioned groups, rather than just the
monopoly AMA (same for Osteopaths) and state licensing
boards, with all required to disclose their training and record of
results on request (the best ones will promote their good
results on their web site, etc.). Pricing is now primarily set by
doctors and dentists exchanging rates so they are all similar,
then they agree on annual increases. This is called 'collusion
in restraint of trade' and is illegal, but the AMA has paid-off the
politicians well.

5) Eliminate dependency on insurance provided by employers.
This is a holdover from WW2 when labor was scarce, wages
were limited by law, and employers used benefits to attract
workers. There is no reason employers should be expected,
much less required by law, to provide health insurance any
more than they should provide food or clothing to employees.

6) Reform our tort laws to reduce excess payments for
malpractice lawsuits that doctors must add to their fees.
Perhaps a special court system for such claims is needed
(similar to bankruptcy).

7) Repeal laws that, a. force (mandate) insurance companies
to offer a long list of covered issues (let people choose the
combinations of coverage they want), 'community rating' and
'guaranteed issue', regardless of existing conditions, age, etc.,
and b. limit operations to a single state. Mandating benefits is
like saying to someone in the market for a new car, 'If you
can't afford a Cadillac loaded with options, you have to
walk.' The huge price increases for insurance in MA and NY
show the counterproductive results of mandates.

8) Make employer and personal payments for health insurance, or HSA deposits (but not co-pays or non-insured items, or use of vouchers), fully tax deductible.

9) Make government medical licenses optional, so we can have a wide range of private practices and clinics, staffed by 'alternate medicine' folks, Physician Assistants, retired or part-time MDs, etc., to see patients for minor problems, including issuing prescriptions for medicine. This approach will give us hospitals, clinics and private practice offices offering; 'Type A' (full service, lots of equipment and specialists), Type B (moderate skills and equipment), and Type C (low cost, run by PAs and volunteer MDs, etc.; they refer cases to Type A and B as needed). Prices will drop as the AMA cartel gets some much-needed competition. If you prefer a government-licensed doctor to handle minor problems, fine, go to one and pay more. I now hear rumors that the AMA lobby is pushing to require that PAs have a Ph.D. in nursing in order to offer the above services; more restrictions to protect the incumbent 'Cadillac' system and MDs. The above 'A-B-C' plan will also help rural areas and small towns attract a 'care person' where they now have only one person or none.

10) Promote creation of private plans, such as: a) Health Savings Accounts (HSAs), funded by the person or employer (or friends and charity), which would pay for routine care and self-chosen insurance for major illness. Deposits would be tax-deductible, and interest on them tax free. Each person would own their account so there would be no loss if they change jobs or retire, and b) Fixed payment plans (a monthly fee, no gov't subsidies, payable with HSA funds) run by private clinics, under their own rules, that will take care of all 'basic' illnesses. Both approaches; a) have positive financial incentives for all parties (stingy spending, shop for rates, healthy life style, etc.) and 'abuse' due to overspending would go to zero since people would be using their own HSA 'medical fund' and wasting it by poor shopping or self-inflicted health problems would be seen as 'foolish' (or stupid!), b) take the government and insurance companies out of 90% of the sessions with a doctor, and c) wise subscribers would buy high deductible ($10,000 to $50,000) private insurance for major illnesses. Some States might choose to provide this insurance.

11) Make all State and Federal elected officials and employees (in any agency or department) subject to the same health care choices as the citizens. No special plans for health or pensions!

Limited Government and Employer Role
While I prefer the above 11-point private plan, to the extent that government stays involved in health care; a) Each state would design, fund and operate their own plan, with zero Federal control and funding, b) The programs should not pay doctors and control prices, but should fund HSAs.

Having the programs funded and controlled at the state level has two benefits: a) It cannot be funded by fake money created out of thin air by the Federal Reserve, thus forcing fiscal sanity on any tax-funded program, and b) Having control distributed over fifty states reduces the size of the administrative bureaucracy each citizen must deal with, and makes states compete as to soundness (including sustainable funding) of their program.

To the extent that employers stay involved they can fund HSAs. History at firms such as Whole Foods shows that employees are stingy with their account (save for future needs) and tend to care for themselves better (diet, smoking, exercise, etc.) to avoid medical expenses.

Private charity (including free services by doctors and hospitals; like the old days!) will be an important part of care for the poor. This will work because with taxes and fees reduced by the above reforms there will be: a. More donations to charities, and b. Fewer people (about a 90% reduction) who can't afford health care.

Conclusion
Note that none of the above suggestions depends on government rules or control of medical fees or practices. It is an ethical plan because all funding is voluntary and does not use mandatory fees, forced purchases of insurance, or coercive taxing (gang-theft-by-vote). Thus it is a fair, moral, responsible, and sustainable plan.

#5) Should Government Manage the Economy?' , March-2011

http://www.activistpost.com/2011/03/should-government-manage-economy.html#more

There is a Great Divide between economists, politicians and citizen activists about the proper role of government in a nation (the land and people).

On the so-called **Left side** we find the Liberals, Progressives, Marxists, Communists, Fascists, Socialists and Neo-Conservatives who support a paternalistic role of government as Mother-Boss-Owner, using laws, fiscal and monetary policy, and ample fiat money from a central bank in their attempt to produce the ideal society concerning social and economic issues. They all want big government, but have a different list of priorities as to what is right and proper.

On the **Right side**, we now only have the Libertarians and Anarchists (and a few traditional 'Taft-Goldwater' Republicans), who want limited or zero government. Libertarians only want the government to protect our personal and property rights, and not manage our lives, the economy, or the world. The current 'Big Government Conservatives

(Nixon, yes Reagan, both Bushes, and Steve Forbes with Heritage.org) dwell in the middle. The debate among these groups has been active since democratic governments started to replace absolute monarchies in the 1600s.

Mercantilism

All of these groups like 'Mercantilism' (also called 'Protectionism'), as a way to control the economy. I define it as: "*A government policy of increasing the wealth of the government (not the people) by using tariffs to minimize imports, and maximizing domestic production of goods and services by decrees and subsidies.*"

Adam Smith first used the term 'mercantile system' in his seminal *The Wealth of Nations* in 1776.

Supporters of Mercantilism emphasize how it reduces off-shoring of jobs, protects the fiat currency from reduced valuation, creates domestic jobs, and increases the wealth of the nation. This approach requires a complex set of tariffs on imports and subsidies to domestic producers, including monopoly privileges for some firms. What they overlook, or avoid, is the inevitable abuse and damage caused by corrupt and incompetent politicians seeking votes by awarding the subsidies and tariffs to supporters.

The incompetence part shows as the government tries to 'pick winners' in choosing the beneficiaries of subsidies and tariffs to increase domestic production and exports. A myriad of rules are proposed to avoid this damage, but the results are always reduced liberty and less economic success in the nation.

Colonies became popular as sources of tax revenue and 'internal imports' for cheap resources (ores, oil), cheap labor, and products (bananas, coffee) that were not available in the homeland. These empires of colonies, or occupied neighbors, all failed as the colonial residents rebelled against the abuse of foreign taxes, laws, and costs of maintaining control drained the homeland. Empire-USA is now in the failure mode as we see rebellion against our well-bribed puppet leaders in the mid-east nations we control, and our 'policeman and boss' expenses soar worldwide.

Most (99%) economists assume that a nations' currency should be, produced by its central bank, and have no gold backing (redeemability of paper notes for gold). Furthermore, they ignore the effect of the US Dollar being a fiat reserve currency, which means the issuer of the worlds' primary currency (now the USA) never runs out of money to pay for imports, thus leading to excess imports and off-shoring of jobs. And, while it lasts, buyers will accept our newly printed money with minimal impact on its exchange rate.

What most (again, 99%) economists do not consider is that using gold as money provides the automatic balance and braking on excess imports and related off-shoring of jobs, as described in '**Redick's Area Law**' below. Since FDR started his big-spending 'New Deal' in 1933, and economist J. M. Keynes published his book *General Theory of Employment, Interest and Money* in 1936, big government has dominated US politics and academia, especially economists (that's where the jobs and grants are!).The prominent big government economists are Keynes, Stiglitz, and Krugman. As I will show below, the free market does a much better job of achieving sustainable liberty, justice, morality (no coercion, or theft), and prosperity, without subsidies and tariffs, and their inevitable abuse and corruption.

Redick's Law of Area Pricing with Commodity Money

My book *Monetary Revolution-USA* has a section in Chapter 5 on the benefits of using gold as money (stable value, smaller government — no funding by creating money out of thin air — fewer and smaller wars, etc.), but my research for this article has produced a new reason, namely *an automatic brake and balance* to avoid damage by excess imports. I have not found this concept documented elsewhere. I humbly call it 'Redick's Law of Area Pricing with Commodity Money', and define it as:

'In a geographical area that uses a monetary system with a commodity as money, and prices set by weight of the commodity, such as with the gold standard, purchases of 'imports' (at 'world' prices) from other areas would result in a reduction in the money supply (weight of gold) in the Buyer's area if not replenished by sales to other areas. A reduction in supply would make the money more valuable (basic 'supply and demand' would cause a higher purchasing power per unit of weight), and thus prices set by local suppliers would go down and become more competitive with imports. Purchases of imports would decline, and exports would increase.'

Thus, use of a commodity as money eliminates the need for tariffs and subsidies to avoid economic harm to an area. Incidentally, high exports would have the opposite effect, causing inflation in the home area. In this manner, constant 'balancing' occurs in exports, imports, and value of the currency domestically. I welcome comments and suggestions.

Herein lies the balance sought by Mercantilists, except that the government and its inevitable abuse by penalties and favors is not involved. This applies to any size area — region or nation — where the nature of physical money flow and transactions are separate enough from other areas for the 'reduced supply' to be noticed by buyers, sellers, and banks in that area. I estimate it would require a 20 or 30% reduction in supply, and six to twelve months, for the price change to take effect, depending on conditions in the subject area (communications, size, etc.).

In the case where there is no local supplier of an imported product or service (bananas, oil, etc.), the money supply in the buying area will decrease until purchases of: a) optional items (bananas) are reduced or ended, and b) necessities are reduced or alternate local sources are privately developed for necessities (solar or hydro instead of oil, etc.), consistent with the level of exports. Rising prices due to low supply of gold, for instance, will drive the transition due to increased domestic buying. Notice that no government intervention is required.

Conclusion

The nice part of being an advocate for limited government, and free markets is that the results in history show that it always works better for more liberty, peace, prosperity, morals and justice; especially when all the big government side effects (more dependence on government, less personal responsibility and initiative) and unintended consequences are included. There are examples of successful economic and social results (good standard of living and growth, good health care, education, etc.) from big government nations such as Sweden, but these always include a big loss of Liberty through intense control of the people's activity. China is an extreme case where they relaxed many economic restrictions and introduced property rights in 1978, and growth zoomed! But, again, personal liberty is a casualty of such policies.

I like a big supply of Liberty. Those folks who are willing to exchange Liberty for security should emigrate, rather than imposing their self-serving controls on other US citizens.

****

Blank

Blank

D. Info on 'Personal Wealth Management'

Contents: (Format=Article # - Page #; A 'T' after article # means the text is printed, an 'A' means it is online in Dave's archives). To see my archive of articles, go to ActivistPost.com, scroll to the bottom of the Home page, select 'Contributors', then my name.

 #   Page   Title

1T- 119- A 'New Factors in Personal Finance' : Ideas about diversifying with guidance from a Professional Advisor (not a salesman; they push what they get commission on). Names of precious metal dealers and storage services.

2T- 126- A 'Internationalize to Protect & Grow Your Assets': How to convert to the currency of another nation, and 'internationalize' by creating a trust in a foreign jurisdiction. Avoid currency collapse, confiscation, and minimize taxes.

3- 130 Text of Chapter 4 'Investment Strategy' in Daves' book **'How to Protect and Grow Your Wealth.'** It gives names of precious metal dealers, and investment consultants.

Visit Daves' business site at www.SaferInvesting.org

****

#1）New Factors in Personal Finance   , Jan-2013

http://www.activistpost.com/2013/07/new-factors-in-personal-financial.html#more

http://beforeitsnews.com/alternative/2013/07/new-factors-in-personal-financial-planning-2704694.html

Personal Financial Planning is one of the most important things you should do, but it is often overlooked. Today's world has financial risks that have never existed before, so much of the "traditional" planning logic is wrong or has voids. For example, most (over 95%) of investors assume it is appropriate to have their assets denominated in US Dollars (USD) if they are a US citizen. After all, the USD is the world's primary reserve currency (banks hold it as reserves – good as gold -, and any Seller will accept it; when India buys coffee from Brazil, they use USD), and the US is the world's largest economy (and military power), so it must be safe. Wrong! The USD's value has been falling for over 100 years, and is now heading toward a crash in value because other nations are starting to avoid using it, thus reducing the demand that has kept it propped-up before.

Why the US Dollar (USD) is Declining in Value

Let's get practical about loss of purchasing power (PP). Example; how much bread would $1 buy in 1913, 1950, and 2013? Answer, 62% less in 1950, and 95% less in 2013!).

Here are the two major reasons the USD is dropping in PP.

1. Monetary Inflation Causes Price Inflation: "Monetary Inflation" means excessive expansion of the money supply (the amount of cash and credit available) by the government and its' Central Bank (ours is the "Federal Reserve System", the "Fed") which leads to "Price Inflation" (reduced value, i.e., purchasing power, of each monetary unit, such as the "US Dollar"). Since the Fed was created in 1913, the value (Purchasing Power) of the USD has dropped by over 95% due to excessive expansion of the money supply by the Fed (urged by the big-spending U.S. Congress). The fastest rate of dropping has been since Pres. Nixon ended the last ties of the Dollar to gold in 1971. Until then, nations could redeem 35 paper dollars for one ounce of gold. FDR ended redemption by mere citizens in 1933. We can all remember that a family car cost about $2,000 in the '70s, but is about $20,000 in 2013; a ten times increase! The same also applies to meat, bread, and clothes, etc. Housing spiked even higher (until the

2008 crash) due to phony loans, low rates, and easy terms from the Fed and Federal government (Fannie, Freddie, etc.). Thus, investors should be concerned about future losses due to the still-falling USD. The solutions (precious metals, and stronger foreign currencies) are discussed below.

2. The USD is Losing its Reserve Currency Status: Dealers in international transactions always choose a strong currency (or several, with one dominant) for use between all nations because it is more convenient than keeping a supply of money from every nation you deal with. Banks use the same strong currencies for their "reserves" so they are viewed as strong and safe. The French Franc and British Pound held this status in their glory days, but lost it as their empires failed. The USD has been 70% of world transactions since the 1920s, but since the 2008 crash, has dropped to 60%, and is still falling as "Empire-USA" declines, and may crash. We don't have traditional "colonies" but control over 50% of the world with our economic and military "agreements". All empires in history have failed, and all primarily due to: a) the high cost of maintain a widespread military and constant wars, and b) parasitic decadence at home, where people work less and expect the government to care for them using "other people's money".

An Historic Time in World Economics

For the first time in history; a) The primary reserve currency is worldwide (not just in areas it controls as when the British pound was dominant), and b) The currency is not convertible to precious metal (typically gold or silver), so is considered "Fiat", where the issuing government declares its "Face Value" and it can be created out of thin air, as with the fiat USD since 1971. ALL fiat currency in history has failed (become worthless) and **the USD is on this path of decline!** We have created so many new dollars (to pay for wars and welfare) that it is losing its value (purchasing power) and nations and businesses are now avoiding using and owning it, or holding assets denominated in USD. Major nations (in particular

Brazil, Russia, India, China, and S. Africa, the "BRICS", are trading with each other in their own currencies. This is an ominous sign and could lead to the end of the USD as a dominant reserve currency and thus limit our ability to create new money to pay bills. When (not if) this happens, our debt and interest rates (and thus payments) will spike up and the value of the USD could fall by 50% to 80%.

When I ask my friends and investors what they predict for the US economy during the next 20 years, I most often get one of these four scenarios:

1) We will muddle along and GDP will taper down. Our children will have a lower standard of living than we had in the 1900s.

2) There will be a rapid inflation (of the money supply and prices), then a depression, but it's hard to tell when. A few economists think we will have a deflationary depression (falling prices, increasing currency value), but I predict that Congress and the Fed will keep using their QE methods of stimulation by creating more money, which always leads to inflation.

3) Congress will fear a crash and vote to end the US Dollar, and become about 20% of a new world currency (a "basket of currencies") run by the IMF. This means we will no longer be the world's primary reserve currency and thus cannot create money to pay our bills. We will have to raise T-bill interest rates to attract buyers. Debt interest expenses will soar and we will default, but survive. Government spending (at home and abroad) will be cut, those people dependent on personal or corporate welfare (or in the military) will suffer.

4) The President will start a war (any reason or fake event will suffice) so then all bets and debts are off! Russia and China will join forces to fight with whomever we attack. Whether we win or lose, we will emerge broke and in a depression.

In my opinion, the best, and sadly least likely, choice would be for Congress to terminate the Fed and return to the gold standard. This ALWAYS works to bring more peace and prosperity for all (wars of aggression are expensive, so there are fewer or none). The essay **in the link below** shows a detailed plan to implement conversion from our present Fed Notes to "gold-as-money", with private mints, redeemable paper notes, and gold weight as the unit of account.

http://www.activistpost.com/2012/01/convert-usa-monetary-system-to-gold.html#more

Now is the Time to Make Changes

No matter which of the above happens, or some other calamity, the USA is in grave economic peril and it is time to consider protecting your wealth by:

1) Converting your cash, bonds, annuities, CDs, and other assets out of the USD to denomination in a stronger currency (issued by a country with low debt and spending, and a strong economic future, such as resource-based), and

2) Purchasing precious metals as a hedge against losses in the value of currency (metal values tend to go up as currency values fall). Take physical possession of your metals; a) because "paper gold" stocks, and ETFs can disappear or have no "backing", and b) store where the the government can't confiscate it (domestic vaults and banks are easy for them to lock-up). Many investors are concerned about the drop in gold and silver prices since 2011, but they should expect recovery to new highs soon because; a) Governments and central banks fear/hate rising precious metal (PM) prices because they indicate currency values are falling. Thus they intervene in the market by selling some of their gold to distort the supply-demand pricing. FDR created the "Exchange Stabilization Fund" in 1933 for this purpose, and it has been active since 2011, along with other governments, to drive down PM prices, b) Private investors fear the "paper certificates" they own (such as "SPDR Gold Shares", ticker

GLD) have little or no gold "backing" so have been dumping this paper, and buying physical gold ("allocated" with their name on it! or personal possession). The sales of "paper gold" affect the spot price more than purchase of "physical" from dealers, so, along with part "a)" above, the PM prices have dropped, but c) Now that prices are lower, the banks and private investors are buying tons of physical gold (banks to boost their reserves, and people to replace the paper) supplies are short. As this demand continues, basic economics says that prices will rise. Experienced Advisors like Eric Sprott, CEO of **Sprott.com**, are predicting new highs within 12 months or less. Thus, today's low prices should be viewed as a buying opportunity.

3) Talk to a professional Financial Advisor (or 'Planner') to get guidance. Look in the phone Yellow Pages, or ask friends for referrals. The problem here is that most only offer "traditional" advice.

In choosing a foreign currency you must look beyond and beneath today's prices and currency exchange rates, and look at fundamentals such as national debt , spending, and unfunded future liabilities (health, pensions, etc.,) to forecast trends in a nation's economic strength and currency value. Foreign exchange markets determine the market value of one currency vs. others, but this can be deceiving because since 2000 most are falling in value together. These values and trends are ignored by virtually all "traditional" brokers and dealers of insurance, annuities, CDs, stocks, and bonds. This is not surprising since most cannot make commissions by selling precious metals or foreign currency.

All of the firms shown work with metals and currencies, either as Advisors or Sellers of products. Most are "contrarian", and not likely to be mentioned by "traditional" Brokers and Advisors. Search the Internet for others. Many offer newsletters and reports (free and paid).

1. Precious Metal Dealers: Europacmetals.net, JMBullion.com, SchiffGold.com, InvestmentRarities.com,

Apmex.com, Caminocompany.com, Monex.com, JimsCoins.net, Blanchardonline.com, Goldmoney.com, and HardAssetsAlliance.com (click on choices at top of HardAssets home page; also go to caseyresearch.com/2013-gold-investors-guide). The above firms are 'established' and there are many others. (go to the Internet or your phone Yellow Pages). When choosing a dealer, investigate to try and be sure they are reliable. Check their 'premiums' and shipping fees.

2. Precious Metal Storage: Once you own some precious metal (PM), where do you keep it? Most dealers work with domestic or foreign "vault" firms you can use. But banks and commercial vaults are not safe (even overseas) because the US government can use "lockouts", "bank 'holidays", "Bail-ins" like Cyprus, or "forced exchange" for bonds or fiat cash, etc. to prevent access by you. This is "confiscation" (theft?) they claim is legal based on the 1917 Trading with the Enemy Act!). If you keep it in your possession, it must be safe from burglars. Most gun stores sell lockable cabinets. A somewhat bizarre, but useful, choice is to bury your PM in a sealed container in a private place such as your backyard. A two- to four-foot piece of 4 to 6 inch diameter PVC pipe from your local hardware, with end-caps glued on, will work. Plant a bush over it to mark the location. Tell 1 or 2 trusted people where it is in case you die, or forget.

3. Foreign Currencies and Equities: **a.** Euro Pacific Capital, Inc. (**EuroPacificFunds.com**, **EuroPac.net**) is a broker-dealer that offers a variety of services and products, including seven mutual funds they created (for "nation diversity"), and precious metals. They promote geographic and currency diversification. **b. Merkinvestments.com** offers 4 foreign currency funds (**merkfunds.com**), and reports. Also see vanguard.com, **c.** EverBank Financial Corp. (EVER, **Everbank.com**) is a US bank that offers savings accounts in foreign currencies. Find more on the Internet.

4. Consultants and Advisors: a. **EuroPac.net**, and **EuroPacificFunds.com/about** (Asset Management), b. **Hardassetsalliance.com**, and **Caseyresearch.com**, c. **Windrockwealth.com**, **bfi-capital.com**, d. **Sprott.com**, and e. **Fisherinvestments.com**. Some 'traditional' sources of info are; a. **cnnmoney.com/expert**, b. **'101 Ways to Build Wealth'**, c. **marketwatch.com** , **newworldinvestor.com** , and d. **theprudentspeculator.com**. Find more on the Internet.

The key point is; "How much will your dollars buy when you eventually cash-in these 'traditional' investments if prices have gone up faster than your investments?" Everyone born after 1933 (now 80!) has always lived with "price inflation" caused by excessive "monetary inflation" (new money and credit issued by the Fed), so tends to treat it as normal. The bad news is, all factors (USD value, spending, debt, wars) point to things getting worse, ending in a possible crash of 50% or more in the USD value!

If the USD loses its reserve currency status (which I think is 90% likely in 1 to 10 years), its value will crash and prices (in USD) will soar. Wise managers of their personal and family assets will study the above issues carefully, and make changes before it is too late. Good Luck!

I repeat, on Oct. 1, 2016 the IMF will make the Chinese Yuan part of their basket of currencies called the SDR (Special Drawing Rights) used like money between nations and central banks. This is expected to cause a fall in demand for USD, and thus a reduction in its' exchange rate and purchasing power. This should cause the price of precious metals to increase.(Update; More in article on p.81)

Dave Redick is CEO and Chief Economist for **www.SaferInvesting.org** *(which offers information, not advice).*

#2) Internationalize to Protect and Grow Your Assets; Jan-2014

http://www.activistpost.com/2014/01/internationalize-to-protect-and-grow.html

Introduction

This article is designed for investors who are willing to look beyond the asset diversification recommendations issued by 'traditional' banks, brokers, and financial advisors (usually all in U.S. dollars), and consider the added diversification of 'Internationalization' by converting most of their assets into safer foreign currencies, trust arrangements, and nations. The expected benefits would be lower taxes, few or no capital controls, low risk of confiscation, multi-generation succession, and worldwide investment choices. I hope this article helps you grow and protect your assets

Most governments worldwide are adding new laws and methods to increase their revenue as they approach economic collapse due to excessive debt and spending. FATCA becomes effective July 1, 2014 and will restrict export of capital, and broaden tax 'grabbing', etc. The USA condition is 'worse than Greece', but we have postponed our crash since the US$ is the world's primary reserve currency (but falling) so we can still pay our bills by creating new money. The best way to protect your assets is to set up a foreign investment trust to own and manage them. This will minimize taxes and avoid capital controls and confiscation. This has happened many times. A more simple way to get partial protection is to buy stock in foreign firms (preferably not denominated in USD) and store your precious metals abroad. The info below will give you ideas. Notice; 'I am not a licensed Financial Advisor'. This is just info to help you develop a plan.

You are Hereby Forewarned of the Possible Collapse of the US$ and Economy!

Jeff Berwick, CEO, tdvmedia.com, said it well:

"If there has been a more dangerous time for your wealth in human history we are unaware of it. There have been individual or even entire nations of people who have been wiped out in the past but never before has there been such risk to assets across the entire globe. … what happens when the US dollar, the world's reserve currency, and all other fiat currencies collapse? It's not if but when. Anyone who has done any research into the financial state of affairs of the western nation-states knows that it is not only inevitable but imminent. And those who have studied the history of currencies, specifically fiat currencies (not redeemable for gold), know that they all eventually reach their intrinsic value of zero and rarely ever last more than forty years, an anniversary that passed on August 15, 2011 which marked forty years since Nixon took the gold backing away from the dollar."

Key Issues

In addition to the traditional investment diversification of asset classes, the concept of 'Wealth Management' considers protection from;

1) The ongoing decrease in **purchasing power** (PP) of the US$ (as revealed in pricing of goods and services, and foreign exchange rate), and

2) The threat of increased taxes, capital controls, and confiscation by the U.S. government.

This article offers two approaches;

1) 'Internationalization' of assets into nations with strong economies, low capital controls and taxes, and a stable monetary and legal system, and/or

2) Creation of a 'Multi-Generation Succession Program', managed by an 'International Business Corporation', and use of 'Charitable Trusts' for tax minimization.'

I define **'Internationalize'** as; "The process done by investors who are concerned about decline of their domestic currency values, and increased taxes, capital controls, and confiscation. At a minimum, they convert their assets to denomination in a stronger foreign currency in an 'investor friendly' country, but this does not help minimize U.S. taxes, etc. A more complete approach is to work with a professional (lawyer, accountant, Wealth Management Financial Advisor) to set up an International Business Company (or Limited Liability Corporation), a tax minimization trust, and banking, in one or more offshore jurisdictions (nations)".

This approach requires a Wealth Management Plan which considers the economic trends and monetary and fiscal policies of many nations, and which ones to deal with based on whether the PP of their currency, and value of real estate and securities is likely to rise or fall.

Wise investors will study the history and problems of our monetary system (this aids investment thinking), and then consider non-traditional strategies (mostly avoid the US$!) to increase their wealth, and reduce risk and taxes by internationalizing their assets with a Wealth Management Plan. See my prior essays at these links;

1) Save the USA by Restoring Government to its proper Role'; http://www.activistpost.com/2011/04/save-usa-by-restoring-government-to-its.html#more ,

2) Empire-USA is Crashing: Loss of Power Over Nations Abroad; Broke and Decadent at Home, Sep. 5, 2013, **http://www.activistpost.com/2013/09/empire-usa-is-crashing.html#more,**

3) How to Abolish the Fed and Convert to Gold as Money, http://www.activistpost.com/2011/01/how-to-abolish-fed-and-convert-to-gold.html#.

#3) Sources for Safer Investing: Text of Chapter 4 'Investment Strategy' in Daves' book **'How to Protect and Grow Your Wealth.'**

1. Precious Metal Dealers: SchiffGold.com, GoldSilver.com, JMBullion.com, InvestmentRarities.com, JimsCoins.net, Caminocompany.com, Monex.com, Blanchardonline.com, HardAssetsAlliance.com (click on choices at top of HardAssets home page), MilesFranklin.com, APMEX.com, Gainesvillecoins.com, Goldmoney.com, SwissAmerica.com, sgpmx.com, and NWTmint.com. There are many others.

2. Precious Metal Storage: Once you own some precious metals (PM), where do you keep it? Most dealers work with domestic or foreign 'vault' firms you can use. Some have their own (**sgpmx.com**). But most banks and commercial vaults are not safe (even overseas) because the U.S. government can use 'lockouts', 'bank 'holidays', 'Bail-ins' like Cyprus, or 'forced exchange' for bonds or fiat cash, etc. to prevent access by you. This is **'confiscation'** (theft?) they claim is legal based on the 1917 'Trading with the Enemy Act'!). If you keep it in your possession, it must also be safe from burglars. Most gun stores sell lockable cabinets. A somewhat bizarre, but useful, choice is to bury your PM in a sealed container in a private place such as your backyard. A two to four foot long piece of 4 or 6 inch diameter PVC pipe from your local hardware, with end-caps glued on, will work. Plant a bush over and tell 2 trusted people where it is in case you die, or forget.

3. Precious Metal Mines: These are high risk/reward investments. Credible sources for info are:

a. Doug Casey CEO of Caseyresearch.com, and his staff, are world experts on PM mining; see Caseyresearch.com .

---

b. 'Streetwise Reports' publishes 'The Gold Report', that includes info on mines at; **theaureport.com/pub/htdocs/38**.

c. Mining.com offers 'Global Mining News' and issues free reports on mining minerals and precious metals.

d. The 'World Mining Congress' (**http://www.wmc.org.pl/**) has members worldwide and holds annual conventions.

e. The 'World Gold Council' (www.gold.org) is a non-profit association of the world's leading **gold mining** companies, that promotes the use of gold. It publishes production data and holdings (tonnes) by nations and banks.

4. Foreign Currencies and Equities:

a. Euro Pacific Capital, Inc. (EuroPacificFunds.com, EuroPac.net) is a broker-dealer that offers a variety of services and products, including seven mutual funds they created (for 'nation diversity'), and precious metals. Look at all parts of the above EP sites for details. They promote geographic and currency diversification. (Note: Europacificbank.com cannot be used by US citizens)

b. Merkinvestments.com offers 4 foreign currency funds (merkfunds.com), and reports. Also see vanguard.com

c. EverBank Financial Corp. (EVER, Everbank.com) is a U.S. bank that offers savings accounts denominated in foreign currencies. The EverBank 'Evolving Economies' Certificate of Deposit (CD) diversifies your money into a basket of currencies that get stronger as the dollar declines.

d. For exchange rate info, transfers, and brokerage, see Forex.com and usforex.com.

5. Wealth Management Consultants and Advisors

a. TDV Media & Services, LLC (tdvmedia.com) was started by Jeff Berwick, CEO, with The Dollar Vigilante newsletter and has grown to a family of services. Michael C. Ross is

President of Michael Ross Consultants Ltd., ABM Management Corp., and TDV Wealth Management Inc., which is an international joint venture between TDV Media & Services LLC and ABM Management Corp.

The **Wealth Management Services** group guides investors into international diversification of assets based on creating an International Business Companies (IBC), Multi-Generation Succession Program, and a Charitable Trust for tax minimization, all developed by their Wealth Management professionals to suit each client. (Notice: I am a Sales Associate for TDV-WM. Please contact me at **Dave@SaferInvesting.org** to schedule a presentation, and on request a price quote. Thanks). Also see **dollarvigilante.com**, tdvgoldentrader.com, goldoutofdodge.com (a $45 report), tdvselfdirectedira.com, tdvoffshore.com, bulletproofshares.com. dollarvigilante.com/homegrown, and tdvpassports.com.

To help implement internationalization, the staff at tdvoffshore.com offers professional services for clients seeking to set up International Business Companies (IBCs), Limited Liability Corporations (LLCs), Trusts and banking in various offshore jurisdictions. There are many reasons to incorporate offshore and numerous great options for TDV Offshore clients to take advantage of, but it is of the utmost importance to understand the wants and needs of those seeking to pursue such things to insure the proper jurisdiction is chosen.

b. There are a variety of 'traditional' sources at cnnmoney.com/expert. See '101 Ways to Build Wealth' at: **http://money.cnn.com/magazines/moneymag/101-ways-build-wealth/**. Also look at **marketwatch.com** , **newworldinvestor.com**, and **theprudentspeculator.com**. Find more Advisors on the Internet; Search for 'Barrons 40 Largest'.

6. Popular Bullion Coins

As a partial step toward using precious metal coins again, the 1933 law that prohibited private ownership of gold coins and bullion was repealed in 1975. Since 1986 the US Mint (www.usmint.gov) has issued a variety of gold, silver, and platinum bullion coins. Their face values are far below their bullion market value, and thus, though they are legal tender, are not used in commerce. Many other nations offer bullion coins. When the US$ crashes, pre-1965 US silver coins and popular government-issued bullion coins, will be usable as money (by weight) because Sellers will know their content.

Bullion coins posture the owners to use them at bullion value if Congress ever repeals the legal tender laws and allows use of private mints and coins. See former Rep. Ron Paul's HR-4248. Many US dealers sell the bullion, medallions, and rare coins, and bars issued by various countries and private mints. See Table on p. 91 for info on weight units.

Summary

If the above issues seem important to you, and my ideas make sense to you, do your homework, then create your plan. If you own over $500,000 in assets, it will pay to work with a professional Wealth Manager to create a sophisticated plan to help you and your children enjoy more wealth, and less risk and taxation. For more information and details, get my book '**How to Protect and Grow Your Wealth**' at Amazon.com.. Table 1 on p. 91 will help you understand coin and bullion weights and fineness. I wish you Good and Safer Investing!

Best regards,   Dave Redick

(**For updates to above articles #2 and #3 visit Chapter 4 'Investment Strategy' in Daves' book 'How to Protect and Grow Your Wealth'** at Amazon.com. **Visit Daves' business at; www.SaferInvesting.org.** This offers information for education, not advice.)

Blank

Chapter 2: Daves' Issue Positions

All of the issues discussed below are part of my '**Restore the USA' plan**. I comment on 33 topics below, but there could be many more. Send suggestions and comments to me at **Redickd@aol.com**.. Thanks.

Most of the statements below are lengthy in order to be complete. However, if you just read the first 10 or 15 lines, you will know the main points.

Contents of Chapter 2:

Issues

For information on other issues, please contact me at **RedickD@aol.com**. I appreciate your interest.

****

1. The Constitution:

 We have observed many examples of people (including some in government who should know better) treating the Constitution as a set of laws and rules that control citizens. Wrong! **The purpose of the Constitution is to: a) define what the government must, may, and may not do, b) plus a list of 'enumerated powers' and restrictions to control their actions**. Congress (the Legislature) makes the laws! That's one of the reasons the 18th amendment (alcohol prohibition) was wrong, it put restrictions on the people. The same applies to a proposed amendment for abortion. Such issues should be passed as laws at the state level, or not at all (if unconstitutional, or none of the government's business, as is true of most things). It is the job of us citizens, and our elected 'leaders', to maintain those limits and keep the government (at ALL levels) on a short leash. The intent was, 'if it is not on the list, the government can't do it!' Many Founders, led by George Mason, balked even at this restraint. They didn't trust the government (and its power-seeking elected members) to stay within the limits, so they wouldn't support ratification until a 'Bill of Rights' (the first ten amendments) to protect the rights of the people and States was included. They were right! The Constitution has been abused to gain power for Federal politicians and their friends. Today, more than half of laws and spending are unconstitutional. Abuse of the 'implied powers', 'general welfare', and 'interstate commerce' provisions account for most deviations. A further misunderstanding is that we are a Democracy. Wrong. In a Democracy the citizens vote directly to make laws, and tyranny of the majority soon rules. We are a Constitutional Republic, where we vote for Representatives who in turn are restricted by the Constitution.

A 'short leash' is required on government power at all levels
(city, county, state, federal) because we grant them 'police
powers' (legal use of force by police and military) which is
easily abused. The current 'War on Terror' and 'Patriot Act' are
good examples of abuse.

2. Dave's Core Principle:

Most elected officials take positions based on their feelings,
personal preferences, and pressure from the special interest
groups who give them money or votes. All of my positions are
based on an objective principle, which is:

"The proper role of government is to PROTECT the personal
and property rights of its citizens, as INDIVIDUALS, from
violation or threat by OTHERS."

With this approach, government ownership and control is
minimized, and human interaction is more peaceful and
voluntary (it pays to get along!), and has a proven track record
of producing more liberty, peace, prosperity, morality, and
justice, proportional to the extent it is employed.

If so, why do people support 'more-government' systems known as Progressive, Liberal, or Socialist? The key is they hope to fund their projects with 'other people's money' by 'tax the rich' schemes. While popular (most people like to have others pay for their benefits), these systems use inherently immoral and coercive 'gang theft by vote' taxation, which results in declining peace, productivity, and justice, if you count all the side-effects (including robbing 'the rich' by forced payment of their so-called 'fair share'). Liberals-Progressives purposely ignore that the top 10 percent of income earners pay about 70 percent of all federal income taxes though they earn only 43 percent of all income. Isn't that enough?? The bottom 50 percent pay only 2 percent of income taxes but earn 13 percent of total income. About half of tax filers paid no federal income tax at all. Note it is 'dollars' that count, not 'percentages'! A society that broadly accepts this type of immoral funding is in decline, as shown by falling morality in all parts of US activity since the 1950s. Sad!

Key points to understanding and using my Core Principle are: a) Our Federal and State governments were created by, and are still controlled by, 'we the people' to protect our rights (a short list of 'natural rights' you are born with, which does not include subsidized or free health care, education, etc.). Thus, the government is our servant, not our owner, manager, funder, or nanny. To implement this protection (enforce the laws), we grant the government 'police powers' (the right to use force), and thus we need to be ever on guard to avoid abuse, including use of laws beyond their intended purpose (RICO, FISA, etc.). For individuals, the flip side of this is; "A person should never initiate force except in self-defense", or "Persons can do whatever they want to, short of violating the equal rights of others". In a personal (not legal) context, I suggest that each person has a moral obligation to be a beneficial presence in the world, and not offensive to others. This starts with being honest, kind, courteous and clean.

Personal rights are freedom of religion, speech, etc. Some of these are listed in the Constitution, but in fact all are 'natural' at birth, and not bestowed by the government (which can only protect or abuse them; not create, except for contrived 'legislated' rights). Our Founders debated if any should be listed (to avoid exclusion of some not listed), hence they included Amendment IX. Note that only a human individual has personal rights.

Notice that 1. Words like 'manage our money, social system, and economy', 'mother', and 'police the world' are not included in the Principle, and 2. We are not 'created equal' as to mind, body and circumstances, but all citizens have equal rights under the law.

Property includes tangibles, and intellectual property owned by a person or legal organization (corporation, etc.). Except for government restrictions (often unconstitutional), a property right is; " The right to use and dispose of your property (use, sell, loan, lease, give, etc.) however you see fit, short of violating the equal rights of others."
Property rights need to be treated as superior to personal rights in order to avoid conflicts. For example, if you enter someone's property without permission (trespassing) and start to give a sermon, your freedom of speech and religion are not being violated if you are made to leave.

b) The government needs police, courts, and military for national DEFENSE to do its job, all used within the limits of the Constitution. But note that the military must not be used to enforce or solve political or economic issues abroad, when there is no threat to our homeland (such as the Vietnam, Iraq, Afghan and Libyan wars).

c) There are no group rights (by sex, race, age, etc.). Every citizen has the same rights. We should not create 'preferred minorities' with special privileges, which are easily abused.

There should be no subjective versions of laws, such as a 'Hate Crimes'. Theft is theft, murder, is murder.

d) Nothing can be a right if you expect someone else to pay for even part of it (such as health, education, etc.). Insurance is a method to share risks and expenses, but must be voluntary, or if run as a 'single payer' by the government, have equal benefits to all, based on terms and payments, and not include a 'welfare' aspect where some members pay less for the same coverage. For example, using property tax to pay for public schools is a rip-off of owners since there is no connection to whether the payer has kids in school (but it is convenient politically!).

e) Your body is your property. If you hurt yourself, or put yourself at risk, it is none of the government's business. Note that the Core principle above ends in 'by others'.

f) The same principle of 'protection' applies to the property rights of business and other legal entities.

g) As with people, the government has no authorization to be the 'owner, manager, funder, or nanny' of the 'national economy'. Free enterprise does a great job of supplying goods and services, while government interference (controls, subsidies, etc.) always do more harm than good, if all the side-effects (including inflation and depressions) are counted.

h) Provision of 'essential services' conflicts with the principle of only 'protecting rights', and is a constant threat to limiting the size of government at all levels (city, county, state, and federal). This is where the federal 'General Welfare' clause is most abused. While most should be 'privatized', to the extent these projects (such as education, sewer, water, roads, public health, parks, mass transit, etc.) are unfortunately approved, they should at least be;

1. Charged to users at compensatory rates (user fees, tuition, no subsidies). Again, voluntary private charity can help the truly needy.

2. Built and operated by contractors on a competitive-bid basis. . The main reason the Federal government has become huge, and involved in running or financing so many unconstitutional state and city projects, is that unlike the States and cities, it never runs out of money, thanks to the Federal Reserve piggy-bank of fake money!

i) The above Core Principle refers to 'violation or threat by OTHERS'. The government only has a role to act when such violations or threats are imposed on someone, and they have no choice to avoid it. For example, non-smokers can avoid privately-owned places that allow smoking (bars, etc; just don't go there!), so it would be a violation of the owner's property rights to impose a non-smoking ordinance, but not City Hall (there is only one, and there are times when you are required to go there; no choice), or other government sites. However, while it is improper to use the legal system to impose your personal preferences on others (smoking, religion, zoning, etc.), there is the viable alternative of 'voluntary negotiation.' This means you (or a group you form) approach the bar owners, or your neighbors, and try to make a deal that serves your wants and needs. Bar owners want customers; maybe they will create a non-smoking room. This applies to any situation. It is peaceful and proper, and no 'tyranny of the majority' is employed.

j) The government cannot do things that are illegal or immoral if done by citizens. Sadly, unethical practices (which should be illegal) such as 'progressive' taxation ('tax the rich' at a higher rate) are justified as 'needed' and a method of charging 'fair share', while in fact it is simply 'gang-theft-by-vote'. Why not have the government rob banks, or give guns to the Red Cross and United Way, for fund raising? This violation of rights is 'tyranny of the majority' and cannot be justified because it is 'the will of the people', 'the American way', and done by the government. There are many other examples (military draft, subsidies, legislative favors, etc.).

The maze of 'social engineering' laws that tell us how to live and work do much more harm than good when all the side effects (unintended consequences) are
considered. My approach emphasizes liberty, personal responsibility, and limited government, which is consistent with our American heritage and Constitution, and history shows it results in maximum liberty, peace, prosperity, ethics, and justice.
Look at the conditions in countries around the world with 'big government' (Progressive, Socialism, or Dictatorships) and judge for yourself. Start with N. Korea, Cuba, and the several '.xxstans' (former Soviet Republics).

3. Debt, Taxes and Spending:

These demons of government abuse all tie together! One needs, or feeds, the other. The citizens lose. See my 'Save the USA' plan in Chapter 5 for more details.

A. Debt: Domestic and foreign debts are at record levels, for both persons and businesses. With a 'national' (or 'public') debt of over $16 trillion, the U.S. government is the world's biggest debtor (and this doesn't count the over $121 trillions of unfunded Social Security and Medicare obligations, P.36). Former Chairman Greenspan of the Federal Reserve Bank (Fed) kept interest rates artificially low (not market-driven) from 2000 to 2006 so mortgages were cheap, to 'stimulate' the economy. It is just like taking heroin, and has withdrawal pains when the economy gets 'sick' from mal-investment (too much money chasing deals). People and business borrowed and spent too much of this cheap money, and then the Fed changed policy, so in 2008 we got; 1. A credit 'crunch' (banks have less money to loan), and 2. Increased interest rates that drove-up ARM (adjustable rate) mortgages. This is what caused foreclosures as home 'owners' couldn't meet their increased payments. Alan Greenspan (Fed Chm. from 1987 to 2006) knew he was creating this monster, but did it to keep his job by pleasing his political bosses. I say he should be indicted for malfeasance and fraud! Instead, he is treated like a sage by his accomplices in Congress and Think Tanks. Ben Bernanke (Fed Chm. from 2006 to present) has used 'Quantitative Easing' (Fed-speak for flooding the economy with new money) called QE-1, 2, and 3-Forever as a 'stimulus', but as any Austrian (see Glossary, P. 211) economist would predict, it isn't working!

The money we send abroad to buy imports comes back to buy government debt or U.S. assets (Treasury Notes, T-Bills, golf courses, part of Morgan-Stanley, etc.), but that can't go on forever. The US Dollar (USD) is at risk of collapse due to excess creation of new money by the Fed (called 'monetary inflation', an increase in the money supply, like a balloon; which reduces the purchasing power of all USD).

B. Taxes: Taxes divert money to the government so people and firms can't use it to spend or invest. History shows that the government uses it unwisely, so the economy and standard of living suffer. We must reduce taxes and spending of all types, and abolish most taxes. I say start by cutting tax rates by 50% or more (the Laffer Curve says revenues might drop less). I recommend 'user fees' (school tuition, toll roads, some 'public services', etc.) whenever feasible, and a 'sales' tax (Not a 'Value Added Tax, VAT, which hides the layers involved) to replace the 'Big Six' of income (personal and corporate), property, interest, capital gains, and inheritance taxes. All of these six taxes amount to a 'penalty on success' and targeted gang-theft, plus a double-tax for inheritance. The sales tax is non-intrusive to personal affairs, less 'progressive' (zero or less 'penalty on success'; except that big spenders pay more), has no disincentive to work and earn, and is easy to manage. Again, Liberals-Progressives like to tax 'the rich' to make them pay their 'fair share', but purposely ignore that the top 10 percent of income earners pay about 70 percent of all federal income taxes though they earn only 43 percent of all income. Isn't that enough??

C. Spending
The U.S. economy and dollar are in trouble, and while our DC 'Leaders' are very worried about it, but won't admit it to us regular folks. They start wars to gain control of oil and other nations instead. Federal spending is out of control. All the elected folks in DC are on a 'feel-good', 'vote-for-me' binge of unconstitutional and excess projects including wars, empire building, pork-barrel earmarks, and projects that should be handled by States, or eliminated. I say; 'Cut spending by at least 50%, or more.

4. 911 and the War on Terror

The facts and logic (means and motive) related to the 911 tragedy build a strong case that it was planned by USA and Israeli leaders to create justification for the forever 'War on Terror' and our invasions of Afghanistan and Iraq (for starters). Never forget that; 1) 15 of the 19 bombers who planned and executed 911 were Saudis, and 2) A group of Saudi Royals were allowed to fly out of the US on Sep. 12 even though there was a stop on all flights. Why didn't we invade Saudi Arabia and do a 'regime change' on the despotic royal family? (Hint: We already had a good oil deal with them). The Saudi Royals, old family friends of the Bushes, are hated by their people, and have paid-off their dominant Wahhabi clerics (a militant sect of Islam and operators of radical anti-American/Christian/Jew mosques and Madrasah schools worldwide; these are the guys who like to lash women because they have been raped) with oil money over the years to avoid a revolution. Ignoring Saudi Arabia is your first clue that Bush and his team had a hidden agenda for the War on Terror!

Many well informed, well educated, and sincere people have concluded that the government at least 'facilitated' the 911 attack as a 'trigger' for their plans to invade Iraq and expand 'Empire-USA'. Israeli and DC both wanted an excuse to invade Iraq and Iran. How else does one explain the series of events such as; 1) FBI inputs on pilot training by Arabs were ignored, 2) NORAD planes were not launched, 3) The towers and building 7 fell straight down at free-fall speed (this can only happen by controlled demolition !), plus the towers were a 'tube' design with large vertical exterior I-beams as the main structure. These beams were cut (severed!) at each floor as the towers fell; HOW??, 4) A demolition company was at the tower site the next morning to haul away debris to a restricted site, then ship it overseas for scrap. (this prevented analysis of how the tower exterior I-beams were cut, and was a massive violation of the crime scene), and 5) the debris and damage at the Pentagon were more consistent with a missile than an

airliner crash. The list of suspicious events goes on and on. A further dimension is that the WTC owner, L. Silverstein, faced a huge expense in ridding the towers of asbestos, and had put a big insurance policy on the buildings (with an extra-cost terrorist clause) a few months before 911. For more info, see **www.scholarsfor911truth.org**, and Dr. Paul Craig Roberts Sep-2011 article:
www.globalresearch.ca/index.php?context=va&aid=26520
. The case is not closed!! The 'official' 911 report is full of errors, bias, poor research, and voids. Calling the citizen investigators 'kooks' working on 'conspiracy theories' will not stop discovery of the truth. This contrived justification for the disastrous War on Terror must be exposed so that the War can be stopped.

 If you find it hard to believe that our leaders would lie to start a war, and allow our troops to be killed and maimed for political and economic reasons (not for defense), then review my column 'Wars, and The Lies that Start Them' (published on Sep-2007) in Appendix 1

The Bush team of 'neocons' (former Liberals such as Wolfowitz, Perle, Kristol, Abrams, and Feith who became 'new conservatives' to seek their personal goals; for more information reference the article **"My Alma Mater is a Moral Cesspool"** on the Counterpunch.org website) took advantage of the atmosphere of crisis generated by 911 to create the 'War on Terror' as a general-purpose, and forever, project to implement their plan to use force to gain control of oil and politics worldwide. The result has been an immoral, illegal and counterproductive crusade. The documented information below traces how Bush and his team got us into this mess and why it will be costly, or impossible, to correct it. All information is verifiable from multiple sources.

The purpose of Clinton's Balkans war was; 1. To gain control of the Balkans region so we could build oil pipelines through it, 2. Build huge Camp Bondsteel as a regional supply center and airbase, and 3. To evict China from Eastern Europe and its oil, including the Caspian area. Remember the 'accidental' bombing of the Chinese embassy in Belgrade? Why was NATO involved when no NATO member had been attacked? Bush's invasion and occupation of Afghanistan was primarily to get access to build an oil/gas pipeline from Turkmenistan and Uzbekistan to a warm water port near Karachi, Pakistan (the same reason the Russians invaded in the 1980's; Google 'Afghanistan, Unocal'). This project had been delayed for many years but was suddenly approved in Dec-2001.

On June 22, 2008, Eric Margolis, Mid East expert, and former Toronto Sun journalist (ericmargolis.com), issued the article: 'These wars are about Oil, not Democracy' which tied together the various political, economic, and oil/gas issues as follows (excerpts): "PARIS -- The ugly truth behind the Iraq and Afghanistan wars finally has emerged. Four major western oil companies, Exxon Mobil, Shell, BP and Total are about to sign U.S.-brokered no-bid contracts to begin exploiting Iraq's oil fields. Saddam Hussein had kicked these firms out three decades ago when he nationalized Iraq's oil industry. The U.S.-installed Baghdad regime is welcoming them back. Iraq is getting back the same oil companies that used to exploit it when it was a British colony.

As former Fed chairman Alan Greenspan recently admitted, the Iraq war was all about oil. The invasion was about SUV's, not democracy.

Afghanistan just signed a major deal to launch a long-planned, 1,680-km pipeline project expected to cost $8 billion. If completed, the Turkmenistan-Afghanistan-Pakistan-India pipeline (TAPI) will export gas and later oil from the Caspian basin (Turkmenistan) to Pakistan's Arabian Sea coast where tankers will transport it to the West.

The Caspian basin located under the Central Asian states of Turkmenistan, Uzbekistan and Kazakkstan, holds an estimated 300 trillion cubic feet of gas and 100-200 billion barrels of oil. Securing the world's last remaining known energy El Dorado is a strategic priority for the western powers.

But there are only two practical ways to get gas and oil out of land-locked Central Asia to the sea: Through Iran, or through Afghanistan to Pakistan. Iran is taboo for Washington. That leaves Pakistan, but to get there, the planned pipeline must cross western Afghanistan, including the cities of Herat and Kandahar.

PIPELINE DEAL: In 1998, the Afghan anti-Communist movement Taliban and a western oil consortium led by the U.S. firm Unocal signed a major pipeline deal. Unocal lavished money and attention on the Taliban, flew a senior delegation to Texas, and hired a minor Afghan official, Hamid Karzai.

Enter Osama bin Laden. He advised the unworldly Taliban leaders to reject the U.S. deal and got them to accept a better offer from an Argentine consortium. Washington was furious and, according to some accounts, threatened the Taliban with war. In early 2001, six or seven months before 911, Washington made the decision to invade Afghanistan, overthrow the Taliban, and install a client regime that would build the energy pipelines. But Washington still kept sending money to the Taliban until four months before 911 in an effort to keep it "on side" for possible use in a war against China.

The 911 attacks, about which the Taliban knew nothing, supplied the pretext to invade Afghanistan. The initial U.S. operation had the legitimate objective of wiping out Osama bin Laden's al-Qaida. But after its 300 members fled to Pakistan, the U.S. stayed on, built bases -- which just happened to be adjacent to the planned pipeline route -- and installed former Unocal "consultant" Hamid Karzai as leader.

Washington disguised its energy geopolitics by claiming the Afghan occupation was to fight "Islamic terrorism," liberate women, build schools and promote democracy. Ironically, the Soviets made exactly the same claims when they occupied Afghanistan from 1979-1989. The Iraq cover story was weapons of mass destruction and democracy.

Work will begin on the TAPI once Taliban forces are cleared from the pipeline route by U.S., Canadian and NATO forces. As American analyst Kevin Phillips writes, the U.S. military and its allies have become an "energy protection force."

Margolis also gave us early warning with his March 2, 2003 article 'Bush's War is Not About Democracy', which said, in part: "Bush's war is not about democracy, weapons of mass destruction, human rights, or terrorism. It has two main motivations. First, the Manifest Destiny crowd in Washington, led by VP Dick Cheney and Defense Secretary Donald Rumsfeld. The terrible events of 911 have seemed to produce an almost psychotic reaction in these good, patriotic Americans, transforming them into 19th century imperialists.

Their intention is perfectly clear: 1) prevent any nation ever challenging U.S. global hegemony; 2) dominate oil. The aggression against Iraq is not about oil per se, it is about control of oil. Before the Iraq crisis, the U.S. imported about $18 billion of crude oil annually from the Mideast, but spent $31 billion keeping military forces there. Why? Control of Mideast oil gives the U.S. domination over Europe and Japan, which draw most of their oil from the region.

Domination of the Mideast and Caspian Sea oil will assure the U.S. a permanent stranglehold over China and India, as well as Europe and Japan.

The second driving force is Israel's far-right Likud government, many of whose ideas have come to dominate Bush administration policy and U.S. media commentary on the Mideast.

The Clinton administration was close to Israel's moderate Labour Party; Bush's camp is totally aligned with Israel's aggressive far right and mirrors its views and policies to a remarkable, unprecedented degree.

Likud and its powerful American supporters want the U.S. to crush Iraq into pieces. The principal beneficiary of the war against Iraq will be Israel.

ADDED BENEFIT: From Washington's viewpoint, the TAPI deal has the added benefit of scuttling another proposed pipeline project that would have delivered Iranian gas and oil to Pakistan and India.

India's energy needs are expected to triple over the next decade. Delhi, which has its own designs on Afghanistan, is cock-a-hoop over the new pipeline plan.
Russia, by contrast, is grumpy, having hoped to monopolize Central Asian energy exports.

Energy is more important than blood in our modern world. The U.S. is a great power with massive energy needs. Domination of oil is a pillar of America's world power. Let's be realistic. Afghanistan and Iraq are about oil, nothing else."
(ericmargolis.com)

Too bad the US citizens and Congress didn't pay more attention to Margolis' prescient words.
On May 13, 2009, Pepe Escobar wrote a fine piece tying together all the pipeline activity and war-politics in the greater Mid east with his: 'Pipeline-Istan: Everything You Need to Know About Oil, Gas, Russia, China, Iran, Afghanistan and Obama' (see **www.alternet.org/story/139983**). It shows how oil dominates all the major military and political activity there, including the USA invasions and wars in Iraq and Afghanistan. This again confirms that the War on Terror is mostly a false-front to justify invading and controlling greater Mid East countries (from the xxstans to N. Africa; Libya, Mali next?) to get their oil.

Iraq never threatened the US and Saddam was not a cohort of Osama. As stated by former US Treasurer Paul O'Neill, Bush and his team had been planning to invade Iraq well before 911. Bush fired him for his lack of 'loyalty', as discussed in O'neill's book 'The Price of Loyalty'. For further insight on Iraq, visit the '**A War in Search of a Reason**' column by Ivan Eland. Thus, they started building a case for preemptive war by fabricating phony reasons such as WMDs and branded Iraq as a part of 911.
In his 'Letter to the American People' in Nov-2002 (see guardian.co.uk/world/2002/nov/24/theobserver), Osama bin Laden stated that his reasons for opposing the USA

were; 1) US bases in Saudi Arabia, 2) extreme US support of Israel, 3) bombing of Iraq for ten years, since 1991, and 4) support of the corrupt Saudi royal family and sale of oil at low prices, denominated only in US dollars (a deal made by FDR in 1945, and Nixon in 1970). Here is the Sept. 28, 2001 interview in which bin Laden states his was not involved with the 911 attack; ummatpublication.com/2012/11/25/). As shown in the Margolis quote starting on P. 148 above, Osama was our 'friend' until in 1999 he helped Argentina get the pipeline deal through Afghanistan, so became our enemy! By early 2011 we had decided to invade Afghanistan and 'take' the pipeline deal. Hence our quick invasion on Oct. 7, 2001, 26 days after 911 ! Such a major military action required many months of planning, so the plans must have been ready!

A study done by Prof. W. Pape at the University of Chicago, and part of his book 'Dying to Win', shows that the primary reason driving suicide terrorists is opposition to occupying troops in their homeland (not religion), which we had done for many years in Saudi Arabia. Yet Bush pushes the fabrication that 'they hate our way of life' as a diversion from the truth. On Dec. 30, 2005 Dr. Paul Craig Roberts, Assistant Secretary of Treasury under Reagan, wrote, "Bush claims that his war crimes are justified because they are committed in the name of 'freedom and democracy'. The entire world rejects this excuse. Sooner or later even Bush's remaining Republican supporters will turn away in shame from the dishonor Bush has brought to America." On Jan. 16, 2006, in his excellent essay on how our Executive branch is becoming dictatorial (**http://www.lewrockwell.com/roberts/roberts139.html**), Dr. Roberts wrote, " It is paradoxical that American democracy is the likely casualty of a "war on terror" that is being justified in the name of the expansion of democracy."

The TRUE REASONS Bush invaded Iraq are:
1) Control of oil (a step to control the greater Mid East),
2) Defense of Israel (plus access to water, oil, and more land for them),

3) Land for permanent bases (hence they had no 'exit strategy'; we built a huge embassy, plus four large airbases and many smaller ones), and
4) Defense of the U.S. dollar (Saddam had converted to selling oil in Euros; we reversed that the day after our invasion).

Also, the Christian Right has a religious reason for insuring the special treatment of Israel, since they believe Israel must exist in order to allow the second coming of Christ. Faith-based persons of influence who favor special treatment of Israel in US policy are Bush, Tom DeLay, John Ashcroft and various church leaders from whom Bush wants support.

In Jan-2006 the sabers started rattling to justify bombing Iran, and are getting louder today in Jan-2013. The 'official' reasons may be different, but the Real Reasons will be the same as three of the above for IRAQ (oil, Israel and defense of the US Dollar). Iran has announced plans to sell oil in Euros. Israel bought 100 'bunker-buster' bombs from us in Nov-2004 (just after the election), and is ready to use them.
The vast 'War on Terror' was created primarily as a cover to give U.S. empire builders the authority to increase their control by meddling in the affairs of other nations worldwide (which just creates new enemies), and restrict objections at home. The 'USA Patriot Act' gives the government excess authority, which is easily abused. Under it, even US citizens tend to be viewed by authorities as 'guilty until proven innocent', and are at risk of being secretly spied upon, or arrested, as terror suspects if they criticize government conduct and policies. All these programs continue with no end, or net benefit, in sight.

A better solution is to stop interfering in the internal affairs of other nations so that we don't create enemies.

As noted above, the primary cause of suicide terrorist attacks is the presence of occupying troops. We should withdraw from our immoral, illegal, and counterproductive ventures in Afghan and Iraq, and most of our bases in over 130 countries worldwide. Bush and his team don't want to withdraw from anywhere because they want to control these places, thus control more oil (and deny it to China), and continue building an Empire worldwide. I believe in strong defense, but not costly and useless wars for Empire-USA that can be avoided with no harm to us.

To help stop our warmonger 'leaders' from starting more wars, we should convene a valid/honest investigation of 911 (with subpoena powers, etc.) and to determine who set it up and 'pulled' the trigger for the explosions. Making our past 'leaders' accountable (and maybe put in jail) will help stop such treachery in the future. Let's get started!

5. How Oil, War, 911, and the US Dollar are Tied

There is a cause-and-effect connection between oil, value of the US Dollar, and 911. The two huge problems, shown in A. and B. below, were known by the Bush Team when they entered office in Jan-2001. They had a warfare plan to control oil and politics worldwide, but 911 gave them cover to get started sooner and bigger.

A. Risk of Collapse of the U.S. Dollar (USD): The value of the USD is now propped-up in part by the fact that most oil sales (to any buyer) are denominated in the USD. The market value (purchasing power) of all fiat currencies (just paper; no gold or silver content or redeemability) depends on the willingness of others to use it (market demand), and hold it as savings, or for a nation, as foreign exchange reserves (typically in the form of US government bonds). All transactions are part of demand, but oil purchases are one of the largest and most visible. A major shift to use of another currency, such as the Euro, would cause a drop in USD value, and could trigger a panic to get rid of USD holdings (cash, bonds, real estate) by foreign persons and nations to avoid major loss of value (30 to 50 percent, or more). China has already started, and S. Korea has hinted. Japan could be next. These three countries are the biggest holders of USD denominated assets. A USD collapse would cause a major US depression, and affect others worldwide.

A shift to the Euro (or any other non-USD currency) by other countries for; 1) Oil purchases, 2) Investments (bonds, businesses anywhere, etc.), or 3) Foreign currency reserves, would reduce support for the USD and is a nightmare scenario for the US.
In Nov-2002 Saddam converted to Euros, which we reversed just after the Mar-2003 invasion. Venezuela is threatening to convert. Iran started its own 'Bourse' trading exchange in early 2007 to compete with existing US and British exchanges, and trades in multiple currencies, including the USD, Euro, and Yen. The shift to Euros puts these countries on top of the list for intervention by the US. The CIA plot to unseat Venezuela's Pres. Chavez in Apr-2002 didn't work, but he is on notice.
My Solution: The USD is vulnerable because of; 1) Excess expansion of the money supply ('Inflation', to pay government bills), and 2) Excess spending and debt by the government. Reversal of these errors will bring strength.

B. Loss of Oil and Gas Control to Russia, China and India:
The oil industry agrees that within about 20 years the earth will reach 'peak oil' production. This means the wells for cheap oil (easy to reach, pump, and refine) will start producing less ('peak oil'). There will be lots of oil left (tar sands, shale, etc.), but it will be very expensive to acquire and refine. The US is competing with other countries (mostly China and India; Russia has its own) for control of the remaining cheap oil. They are traveling the world together to negotiate long term contracts (China announced one with Saudi Arabia in Jan-2006). The U.S. is invading oil producers on false pretenses to gain control. Russia's long dispute/war in Chechnya is mostly about control of oil, gas, and pipelines in the Caspian region where Russia seeks broad control. India and China face oil

shortages in the future so they are cooperating in deals to gain control of oil in the Mid East, Africa and SE Asia. This threatens US availability and price of over 80% of the world's proven 'cheap' reserves. These are key reasons for the US wars in the Balkans, Afghanistan, and Iraq, and threats to Iran. The stakes could not be higher, including risk of broad and long wars, and economic depression, for all nations involved.

Rather than seeking military and political control of oil-producing nations (a costly and immoral method), the US should negotiate long-term contracts for supply. Big customers have clout! This approach will also end creating enemies by meddling in the affairs of other countries.
With the Iraq war not going well, Bush collaborated with the former enemy Sunnis (Cheney's Jan-2006 trip around the region) on a deal to reduce the anti-US attacks inside Iraq so the US can declare victory and get out 'with honor'. Of course the original plan was to stay forever in order to; a) Control Iraq oil, b) Use permanent bases in Iraq to control the Mid East, c) Defend Israel, and d) Keep Iraq oil sales in US Dollars.
Bush's failure to capture Osama bin Laden was no accident. Having him at large helped keep him (and now Obama) as 'War Presidents' so the above issues could be pursued as part of the forever War on Terror. The same applies to onerous checking and restrictions by the TSA on carry-on luggage for air travel, while the checked baggage is barely inspected. This keeps 'the people' on edge about terror, so they will not object to loss of liberties. The illegal and desperate measures (domestic spying, torture, etc.) taken by Bush showed his concern about avoiding new attacks on US soil, which are made even more likely by his ongoing intervention for the above issues in the Mid East.
FLASH - The so-called 'Killing of Osama' in May-2011 by a Navy Seal raid was a staged event to boost Obama's popularity. All insiders believe he died from kidney disease years before. The ultra-phony picture of Hillary, Gates and others watching the raid on TV was a bad joke. The quick dumping of the body at sea, and the convenient death of all

the Seals in a later accident??, are two of the many other well-documented reasons to show the whole event was fake.

I support a strong defense, and wars needed for defense (not for Empire-USA), and approved by Congress. In their effort to solve the above problems and gain power worldwide, I say the Bush Team operated as an Imperial Presidency, with excess use of force and secrecy. They are using: 1) foreign aid, intervention, and war in a plan to control the world's politics and oil, and 2) high spending, funded by debt, to pacify the folks at home. The first version of the warfare plan was secretly issued in Sep-2000 by the 'Project for a New American Century' team (PNAC, a DC think tank) which started in 1997. The plan called for increased military force worldwide to promote control of oil and their special-interest politics. When Bush was elected in Nov-2000, many of the authors (including Don Rumsfeld, Jeb Bush, Steve Forbes, Perle, Kagan, Feith, Abrams, and Wolfowitz: Cheney was a cofounder) joined the Bush team. For details, refer to the 25Feb03 essay, '**The Project for the New American Century**', by William Pitt and Scott Ritter (former UN Inspector for Iraq weapons). As shown by the demise of all previous empires in history, this approach never works. It is a path to military, economic, and ethical failure. Perhaps due to the bad reputation they got from the failed Iraq adventure, the PNAC gang regrouped in May-2009 as 'The Foreign Policy Initiative' (**foreignpolicyi.org) to pursue the same war-based policies.**

6. American Independence and Sovereignty
The U.S. has become entangled in a host of international agreements and memberships that threaten our sovereignty, and could oblige us to go to war to protect other nations. The UN, NATO, and International Criminal Court (ICC) are old ones, but more recently we have joined GATT, NAFTA, CAFTA, and WTO, with TTIP and TPP coming. A looming (and largely secret) threat is the North American Union (NAU),

which some say would essentially merge Mexico and Canada with us (can you say oil?). It involves building a highway from Mexico to Canada, with 'free-wheeling' rights for Mexican trucks and drivers to operate in the U.S. We should withdraw from any deal or orgs that infringe upon the freedom or independence of the USA. Trade is good, but does harm to the USA and its' people when the government gets involved and injects crony capitalism!

A major threat is the anti-American "Law of the Sea" Treaty (LOST), or UNCLOS, was deferred again in July-2012 due to lack of votes, but the supporters keep trying. The LOST convention's purpose is to benefit Third World countries by fining and punishing the wealth and technological advantages of the industrialized West. The convention would subject our governmental, military and business operations to mandatory dispute resolution. Any disputes would be decided by the U.N. International Tribunal for the Law of the Sea, a 21-member body representing 155 countries envious of American ingenuity and prosperity. The United States would have only one vote with which to protect American investment, and the transfer of sensitive, militarily useful and proprietary private technologies, and forced compliance with the Kyoto Protocol.

The LOST convention would be an open invitation to activist judges to interpret the convention's intentionally vague provisions against our national security and economic interests. In point of fact, were our Senate to approve the LOST convention, the odds are roughly 155 to 1 that the LOST tribunal would vote to cede U.S. claims to the North Pole and its oil riches to the Russians.
U.S. adherence to this treaty would entail history's biggest and most unwarranted voluntary transfer of wealth AND surrender of sovereignty. LOST, which was a product of the Left/Soviet/non-aligned movement agenda of the 1960s and 1970s, created the International Seabed Authority (ISA). ISA is a new supranational organization with unprecedented powers to regulate all 'sea' activity!

7. Restitution and Compensation:

'The law of restitution is the law of gains-based recovery. It is to be contrasted with the **law of compensation**, which is the law of loss-based recovery. When a **court** orders restitution it orders the defendant to give up his gains to the claimant. When a court orders compensation it orders the defendant to compensate the claimant for his or her loss.' These are both litigation situations. (en.wikipedia.org)

When the government is the claimant and collects a fine from a lawbreaker, the money is usually kept by the government (another money grab!). I suggest that whenever feasible (the victims are living and known), the victims of the crime should receive the money as restitution or compensation, shared in proportion to the damage they suffered.

8. Health Care

 Liberals/Progressives/Socialists strive for 'free' government-provided health care as a right. Of course, any health care program is unconstitutional, but that means nothing to most Congresspersons and voters. 'Universal Health Care' is another attempt to get 'the rich', or at least 'someone else', to pay for everything they want. I have lived in Canada and experienced the fact that when doctor's training, and then salaries, are paid by the government, 1. There are fewer doctors per 1,000 citizens, 2. Importation of cheaper foreign-trained doctors increases, and 3. The patient **becomes 'more work'** rather than a valued client they want to nurture and keep, and the level of care, caring, and courtesy declines accordingly. Most Canadians value their English roots and view the government akin to 'Mother', thus are patient with her faults, and proud (sometimes with vanity) of their traditions and Royal Family. Many view 'Americans' as relative ruffians, and self-centered , dog-eat-dog predators who don't care for each other. Hence their pride in, and patience with, their health system.

Of course, government budgets are a huge issue as to which and how much services and medicines are available, and to whom (rationing). The medical specialists and equipment for expensive services such as organ transplants are limited, and people wait for years (and sometimes die) waiting. It's the same kind of rationed care you'll find in nations like France and the England, where waiting lists for lifesaving procedures are sometimes years-long, and the death rates from breast and prostate cancer are twice to three times higher than in the United States. You can't see a specialist (ear, eye, skin, etc.) without referral by a family doctor. Old people are sometimes deemed 'not worth it' for expensive treatments and drugs.
It has been illegal in Canada to open a private 'for fee' clinic, since that is deemed unfair to those who can't afford it, but that is changing. Canadian health managers now admit that their system is financially 'unsustainable' (same in France and others), and that formerly illegal 'private services' (non-government doctors who charge a fee) and private insurance will be needed to avoid collapse. Some provinces already allow certain private services, and even pay private hospitals to take care of 'public' patients. At the extreme (Russia, etc.), corruption sets in, and doctors and staff demand bribes for access to services.

In the face of all of the above, Liberals keep pushing for 'universal health care', and they have a friend in Obama. His plan will be announced soon, and is expected to cost billions to taxpayers, with 'the rich' and employers targeted for most of the cost. This source of funding is a ripoff, but upsets fewer voters.

The cost of routine care has skyrocketed since Medicare and Medicaid were started. Health-care spending has increased from 5% to 16% of gross domestic product (GDP). Cost of these programs was the major reason, but part of the price increase is due to; 1. Loss of US Dollar value, 2. The 1986 'Emergency Medical Treatment and Labor Act' (EMTALA) rules that hospitals must give the poor free 'exam and stabilization' service in their Emergency Centers (under the extortive threat of losing their Medicare business), and these unpaid bills are added to those who do pay, 3. Excess payments for malpractice lawsuits (reform of our tort laws is needed), and 4. Collusive price-fixing (minimum rates) set by the state-level American Medical Association (AMA) chapters and their member doctors. Further, the AMA prohibits members from advertising their rates (or skills, and track record of results). If a doctor violates the AMA rules, he/she loses their license to practice, or is harassed out of business (no referrals, etc.)! The federal government would normally attack this practice under anti-trust laws for 'collusion in restraint of trade', but the AMA has political influence, and gets a pass, which we all pay for! Also, as technology and medicines improve, people are living longer, so there are more years of illness and expenses, which often require high cost intensive care and thus higher expenses for each illness. Even young and middle-aged people may incur high expenses if costly new technology and medicines are needed. Un-funded federal mandates for free emergency service at hospitals (the Feds demand compliance or threaten to drop the hospital as an 'authorized' Medicare provider; this is an extortionist violation of rights) is often abused by illegal immigrants, or those that choose to not have insurance, and this causes higher per-day rates (to make up for non-payers) for those persons and insurance firms that do pay their bills.

My Position: I suggest a twelve-part plan aimed at getting the government OUT of patient-doctor-hospital control and funding so that positive free-market incentives guide the patients and doctors:

1) Phase-out Medicare and Medicaid as the lower costs of free-market care become available (as described below, and vouchers in item 12), and start with having higher co-pays on Medicare and Medicaid to give incentive to avoid unhealthy life styles and non-essential visits to, and treatments and tests by, the doctor,

2) Reduce costs by greater use of Physician Assistants (PAs) so a doctor's time is not wasted on routine work the assistant can perform (including clinics run by PAs; see Item 9 below),

3) Use the FDA only to determine and disclose possible side-effects and viability of drugs, but not restrict use of them (or their potency) until there are virtually no side-effects: Let doctor judgment and CONSUMER CHOICE rule!,

4) Bring the lower price and higher quality benefits of competition, and consumer choice into health care by busting the medical pricing cartel and allowing doctors to advertise their rates (web sites ads, etc.), training and results records (see Items 2 and 9; the American Medical Assoc.-AMA- prevents this; same as ABA for lawyers) and practice as members of private, non-government sanctioned groups, rather than just the monopoly AMA; OK there are a few Osteopaths too) and state licensing boards, with all required to disclose their training and record of results,

5) Eliminate dependency on insurance provided by employers. This is a holdover from WW2 when labor was scarce, wages were limited by law, and employers used benefits to attract workers. There is no reason employers should be expected, much less required by law, to provide health insurance (see item 12 below), any more than they should provide food or clothing, to employees. It is just another way to avoid raising taxes (same as free EMTALA hospital service above),

6) Reform our tort laws to reduce excess payments for malpractice lawsuits that doctors must add to their fees. Perhaps a special court system for torts is needed (similar to bankruptcy),

7) Repeal laws that, a. Force (mandate) insurance companies to offer a long list of covered issues (let people choose the combination of coverages they want), 'community rating' and 'guaranteed issue', regardless of prexisting conditions, age, etc., and b. Limit operations to a single state. Mandating benefits is like saying to someone in the market for a new car, "If you can't afford a Cadillac loaded with options, you have to walk." The huge price increases for insurance in MA and NY show the counterproductice results of mandates.

8) Make personal payments for health insurance (but not co-pays or non-insured items) fully tax deductible,

9) Make government medical licenses optional, so we can have a wide range of private practices and clinics, staffed by 'alternate medicine' folks, Physician Assistants, retired or part-time MDs, etc., to see patients for minor problems, including issuing prescriptions for medicine. Prices will drop as the AMA cartel gets some much-needed competition.

This new approach will foster more personal responsibility by citizens (less abuse of the system; less smoking and obesity, etc.), and will give us hospitals, clinics and private practice offices offering; 'Type A' (full service, lots of equipment and specialists), Type B (moderate skills and equipment), and Type C (low cost, run by PAs and volunteer MDs, etc.; they refer cases to Type A and B as needed). This will allow people to check-out their prices, skills and record and make a choice !! With price competition, and no 'mandated coverage' plans, prices will drop, and health and access for all will improve.

If you prefer a government-licensed doctor, fine, go to one and pay more. I now hear rumors that the AMA lobby is pushing to require that PAs have a Ph.D. in nursing in order to offer the above services. YUK!; More restriction to protect the incumbent 'Cadillac' system and MDs.

10) Promote creation of private plans, such as: a) Health Savings Accounts (HSAs), funded by the person/owner or employer, which would pay for routine care and insurance for major illness. Deposits would be tax-deductible, and interest on them tax free. Each person would own theirs so no loss if they change jobs or retire, and b) Fixed payment plans (a monthly fee, no government subsidies) run by private clinics, under their own rules, that will take care of all 'basic' illnesses. Both approaches; a) have positive financial incentives for all parties (stingy spending, shop for rates, healthy life style, etc.), b) take the government and insurance companies out of 90% of the sessions with a doctor, and c) subscribers would buy high deductible ($10,000 to $50,000) private insurance for major illnesses. (Note; This is similar to the voucher system in Part 12 below, but privately financed),

11) Make all State and Federal elected officials and employees (in any agency or department) subject to the same health care choices as the citizens. No special plans for health or pensions!!, and

12) To the extent that government stays involved in health care, it should; a) Be run and funded by each State, with zero Federal control and funding, b) The programs should not pay doctors and control prices, but should, c) Issue quarterly vouchers (useable only for health expenses and insurance) to 'well' citizens and permanent residents (same amount to all), but not to illegal aliens, and let them shop for the privately provided services they need, including both direct payment for routine care and insurance for major illnesses, and d) To help people caught in transition from the old system, issue special vouchers to those with major 'existing conditions' that preclude their purchasing insurance, with payments continuing until the end of their illness, or death. The value of the vouchers would be owned by each person, and could be transferred; a) to their account in another State if they move, b) as a gift, or by a will upon death, to other qualified people, in any State. Having the programs funded and controlled at the State level has two benefits: a) It cannot be funded by fake money created out of thin air by the Federal Reserve, thus forcing fiscal sanity on the tax-funded program, and b) Having control distributed over fifty states reduces the size of the administrative bureaucracy each citizen must deal with, and makes States compete as to soundness (including sustainable funding) of their program.

To the extent that employers stay involved they can fund a 'health savings account' that the employee would own and spend (similar to a voucher). History at firms such as Whole Foods shows that employees are stingy with their account (save for future needs) and tend to care for themselves better (more diet, exercise, etc., and less smoking, alcohol, drugs, etc.) to avoid medical expenses.

Private charity (including free services by doctors and hospitals; like the old days!) will take care of the poor. This will work because with taxes and fees reduced by the above reforms there will be: a. More donations to charities, and b. Fewer people (about a 90% reduction) who can't afford health care.

In conclusion, note that none of the above suggestions depend on government rules or control of medical fees or practices. It is an ethical plan because all funding is voluntary and does not use mandatory fees, forced purchases of insurance, or coercive taxing (gang-theft-by-vote). Thus it is a fair, responsible, and sustainable plan.

****

For more info on health care plans, see:

1) www.pacificresearch.org. Their CEO, Sally Pipes, is from Canada and knows their problems well,
2) An essay from The Independent Institute:
www.independent.org/publications/tir/article.asp?a=740
3) A collection of articles from The Cato Institute:
www.healthcare.cato.org
4) 'A Four-Step Health-Care Solution' written by Hans-Hermann Hoppe in 1993
(**http://mises.org/freemarket_detail.aspx?control=279**)
5) A list of essays on health at Downsize DC, a think tank for 'less government':
http://www.downsizedc.org/bySubject/health6) An analysis of state health programs : 'The Lesson of State Health-Care Reforms' on Oct. 6, 2009 by Peter Suderman of
www.Reason.com . Go to
http://online.wsj.com/article/SB10001424052748703298004 574455560453947646

9. Employee Unions: Unions serve a needed function when they protect members from fraud or abuse (long hours, unsafe conditions, etc.) by the employer. However, once these basic goals are met, the union managers usually try to keep or enhance their jobs (more pay and power) by seeking more concessions in the form of ever higher pay, health and pension benefits, work rules that reduce productivity, etc. As union membership declined in the 1980s, union organizers focused on government workers such as teachers, fire and policemen, prison guards, staffers, etc. (see SEIU.org and AFT.org). Refer to Stephen Greenhut's *BOOK* 'Plunder!, How Public Employee Unions are Raiding Treasuries, Controlling Our Lives and Bankrupting the Nation'.

As noted in Issue # 10 Pensions below, "In many cases, benefits became excessive when self-serving managers 'gave away the store' to avoid a strike..." Thus, there is self-serving abuse by both employer and union managers that lead to excessive costs that hurt profits and growth of the employer, or cause bankruptcy, both of which cost jobs! The US steel and auto industries are examples.

The solution is; 1) The government should not give or allow special privileges to unions to boost their income and membership (such as check-off system for dues, forced union membership when hired –union shop-, guaranteed job after strike, 'prevailing wage' laws, minimum wage, etc.), but 2) Should fulfill its proper role of protecting the rights of citizens (see Issue #2, P. 138), including suits by unions due to abuse of workers by employers.

10. Employer Pensions

An employer has the option of offering a pension plan to employees or not. If offered, there should be written disclosure (dated and signed hard copy) of the rules (co-payments, benefits, age and years of service to retire, restitution of equity upon termination of employment or of the plan, disclosure of fund investments, etc.), and whether the rules can be changed or the plan terminated. Just as with an insurance policy, it is the personal responsibility of the prospective employee to read and understand the plan and decide if he/she wants to work there. In recent years many plans have been changed or terminated (sometimes as part of bankruptcy) by firms in financial trouble. The government created the Pension Benefit Guaranty Corp. (PBGC) to protect workers from loss of pensions. Like most government plans it doesn't work very well. Further, it creates the perverse incentive, or 'moral hazard', of temping firms to take advantage of PBBC. The PBGC disclosed in its annual financial report that as of Sept. 30, 05 it had $56.5 billion in assets to cover $79.2 billion in pension liabilities. There has been an explosion in recent years in the number of big, ailing companies - especially in labor-heavy industries like airlines and steel - transferring their pension liabilities to the PBGC. With billions of dollars flying out of the agency's door, concern has been mounting over its financial footing. In many cases, benefits became excessive when self-serving managers 'gave away the store' to avoid a strike that would; 1) In the private sector, cause loss of profits that would hurt their next bonus, and 2) In government, cause loss of campaign donations and votes. Steve Greenhut tells the story in his book, 'Plunder! How Public Employee Unions Are Raiding Treasuries, Controlling Our Lives And Bankrupting The Nation!' (more on SEIU.org on P. 166, #9)

My Position: A company need not offer a pension plan, but if it does, the rules must be published when an employee joins, and not changed without negotiation. Anything less would be fraud, and breach of contract. The government's only role should be to require full disclosure of the rules noted above, and ongoing disclosure to confirm that the plan is properly funded. The absence of these two forms of disclosure is what has led to the painful loss of pensions by many employees.

11. Social Security

This has been about 20% of the Federal budget and is growing yearly. The present system is a welfare program for seniors, paid to them by current workers. Seniors have no equity (ownership) of the amounts they have paid-in to FICA in their working years (and contributions by their employers) and the government can stop paybacks (checks from the government) to seniors at any time. It is a devious plan and must be reformed before it fails (goes broke due to more recipients than payers) and hurts many people who are planning for it, or already dependent on it. My transition plan is to; 1) Keep the present plan in force for people age 55 or older, make paybacks proportional to amounts paid in (now immigrants get nearly full pay, with a low history of pay-ins), extend start date of payback to age 70, and grant equity ownership for pay-ins made, 2) Reduce payback amounts as needed (due to reduced program income), with five years advance notice, 3) End 'contributions' by employers, and 4) Allow people age 18 to 55 to join the new plan or go 'on their own'. Either way, they will get credit/payment for their prior pay-ins, and interest.

The current program is immoral because it depends on robbing the younger generation for 'contributions' (pay-ins) sent directly to current 'recipients' of paybacks (there is no 'fund', just bonds, –IOUs-), and is unsustainable because costs are rising while 'contributors' are declining in number and income.

My proposed new program below, 'Redick's Private Pension Plan', is similar to the plan in Chile since the hugely successful new version started in 1981 (see; **http://www.cato.org/pubs/policy_report/pr-ja-jp.html**, by José Piñera, who as Chile's Minister of Labor privatized the state pension system, is President of the International Center for Pension Reform and co-chairman of the Cato Institute's 'Project on Social Security Privatization'; Cato.org). My Plan is optional (individuals join if they wish) where citizen contributions would be invested by private investment fund firms chosen by the citizen, and the citizen would own the account equity. Growth in value would be tax free. A government regulatory body would set some broad investment diversification rules, to avoid high-risk or politicized investments by the fund managers. The contribution amount (weekly or monthly; a percent of pretax pay, or other personal funds) would be chosen by the citizen based on his choice of retirement age. This would encourage middle-class and low income people to start an account, which they would normally view as 'only for the rich'. This program has proven very popular in Chile (90% of workers joined!) due to the ownership aspect, which fosters personal responsibility. There are many side benefits such as increasing capital available for investment (by the pension fund firms) which reduces unemployment, plus better social and economic conditions in Chile. Go to the Cato.org link above for more details.

The 'private' and 'personal' aspects of my Plan will lead to more personal responsibility in our society, including more work, saving and good relations with the family and friends who will help care for the aged. Poverty cases can be served by private charity. The attitude of 'the government owes us everything' and 'it's OK to take others people's money to pay for my benefits' will fade. Thus, my plan is both moral and sustainable.

12. States Rights (Federalism): The 'Articles of Confederation' were considered too weak on national defense and other matters, so a convention was called to strengthen them. This evolved to writing an entire new Constitution, which was completed in 1787. At first the States were sovereign and dominate and the new nation was referred to as 'These United States'. This soon evolved to 'The United States of America' and States Rights kept getting weaker, especially when the federal government got control of the monetary system in 1913 with creation of the Federal Reserve System (more below). Our constitution grants enumerated powers (a list; if it's not there, you can't do it) to the Federal government (hereafter 'DC'), and by the 10th amendment, all other powers to the States, or people. Over the years, Congress, the President and courts have twisted the 'general welfare' and 'commerce' clauses of the Constitution, and invented the 'implied powers' concept, to grant enormous powers to DC, including overriding existing state laws. The Founders knew it was good to have differences between states so citizens could 'vote with their feet' if laws and taxes got oppressive. This is why U.S. Senators were to be appointed by their state legislatures, so they would better represent the interests of the states in DC (ended by the 17 th Amendment). Part of the reason the DC involvement has grown is that they control the monetary system (run by the Federal Reserve Bank, 'Fed') and, since leaving the gold standard in 1971, can create money out of thin air! The size of the DC piggy bank is only limited by politics in the short run, and hyperinflation and bankruptcy in the long term, and this why states become dependent on DC money for education, health, police, and many other functions normally paid by the people or state. States love getting this money, and Congressmen love taking credit for them (it's called 'pork' to get votes and campaign donations), but it comes with strings attached ('You must do X or we will stop sending money for Y'). Thus, DC feels free to impose unfunded mandates such as free emergency health care, and immigrants/refugees, on the states, and activate the National Guard (originally State Militia), without the Governor's permission. Now the Dept. of Homeland Security is sending equipment and money to local police so they can do their dirty work. The police love the new money and power!

My position: Federal power and spending must be pushed back. The Fed's have no business in education, overriding state laws, drugs, abortion, police, and a long list of other state and local issues ! The Federal government should not be involved in an issue, unless empowered by the Constitution. See Issues 29 and 30 below for my positions on Nullification and Secession.

13. Privacy and Personal Liberty

A. National ID Card: Support for a national ID card (with the same info imbedded in drivers licenses) is growing and must be stopped. Abuse is inevitable in this type of federal system.

B. Wiretapping: Tell your representative to protect Fourth Amendment guarantees against warrantless searches:

Repeal the Protect America Act. The PAA legalizes warrantless wiretapping of U.S. residents, which the Bush Administration secretly began in 2001, and violates the Foreign Intelligence Surveillance Act (FISA) and the Fourth Amendment. (H.R. 3773 and 3782 would repeal the PAA.)

Restore the requirement for individualized warrants for wiretapping of U.S. communications and email. U.S. Intelligence agencies cannot oversee themselves. The judicial branch has a necessary role in preventing abuses of power. (H.R. 3782 would restore individualized warrants for any wiretap of U.S. calls or emails, whereas H.R. 3773 would permit the wiretapping of some international calls and emails of Americans without individual warrants.)

No immunity for telecommunications companies that broke the law by permitting the government to conduct surveillance of their customers' phone and email records. To grant those companies retroactive immunity condones presidents and private industry collaborating to ransack the public trust. (Neither H.R. 3782 nor H.R. 3773 currently grants immunity, but administration allies may introduce amendments that do so.) Let the public see the text of Congress's bills BEFORE they are passed. Fourth Amendment rights to privacy are among our fundamental and inalienable rights. The specific text of any bill that may affect these rights must go before the American people for comment.

14. Separation of Church and State: Persons of faith sometimes complain that their right to engage in religious activities is unfairly restricted. They say our Founders were Christians, so the USA is a Christian nation. Well, they were also white males; does that make us a white male nation? Solutions are usually sought in the 'Establishment Clause' of the First Amendment, or 'Freedom of Speech'. I say this is the wrong approach since these clauses are only about the government; 1) Not naming and supporting a certain religion (as had been done in Europe and some states), and 2) 'The free exercise' of the religion chosen by an individual. As shown in 'Dave's Core Principle' (item 2 above), property rights need to be superior to personal rights (such as religion) to avoid conflicts. This applies to many subjects and situations.

My position: I recommend a property rights approach. While it is compulsory to abide by the laws of the government where you live, religion is an optional and personal choice of each individual. Laws and rights of others must not be violated in the practice of religion. Our constitution protects us from tyranny of the majority. Thus, religious groups should not attempt to mix government and religion, even when in a majority (or active minority), since it imposes (by force of law for coins, pledge), or insertion into government events and places, owned by all (schools, buildings, prayers at events) their option on others. The U.S. has complete freedom of religion so people can engage in their religion as much as they like on their own time, events, and property. However, just as it would be trespassing for a preacher to enter a private home or event to conduct a service, no religious group can use or adorn property, objects, procedures, or events owned in part by others (such as the government) without the permission of ALL owners (not just a majority), or their authorized agent. This applies to coins, the Pledge of Allegiance, public schools, non-church meetings, displays in government buildings, prayers at public meetings, even if attendance to such events or displays is optional.

A similar issue of trespassing would apply to Islamic mosques using loudspeakers for 'call to prayers' if they create unwanted noise in the neighborhood. The noise should be stopped on the basis of violating the neighbor's property rights ('quiet enjoyment' laws and precedents).
 Bush-43's 'faith based' subsidies to religious groups are an obvious unconstitutional ploy to promote religion, and should be stopped. Further, it harms religious work by making such groups dependent on government handouts, and subject to its rules (strings attached).

Religion obviously should not be part of our relations with other countries as to special treatment abroad, or with their lobbies in the U.S. (can you say Israel and AIPAC?).

15. Education: Today's K-12 government schools offer essentially only one flavor of education. In some districts parents can choose a school, but this offers minimal variation. They all preach 'government approved' mush that promotes government as the source of 'good and nice' things, and hide the many lies, and unconstitutional, criminal acts of the government, at all levels. Administrators have a perverse incentive to promote poorly educated kids to keep them enrolled so the state and federal money keeps coming. Our students test lower than students in European and Asian schools under similar circumstances. A big part of the difference is the poor work ethic we engender in our kids due to lack of discipline, including almost no risk of expulsion for causing trouble.

My position: Education of children is the responsibility of parents as to amount and type. The same benefits we enjoy from a free market in food, cars, etc. (as to variety of types, and cost) would apply if schools were all private (for profit or non-). By paying tuition, parents would instantly 'be involved' to be sure they were getting their money's worth. School administrators would treat students and parents as customers who seek a good service, and can shop around for it! Good teachers would get raises the same way an engineer does (ask if you feel you deserve it, or quit and go to a competitor). They now risk loss of accrued pension benefits, but this would not apply under my plan in item 10 above. Good teachers attract customers. Parents would monitor curriculum content and teacher quality and negotiate for changes, or leave. Poor quality schools would be exposed by independent testing services or college entrance exams. This would reduce incentive for administrators to engage in grade inflation, because they would get caught.

I say we should, 1) Allow creation of private nonprofit schools without government license or controls (except fraud, a proper government issue), 2) Phase-out property taxes as a source of revenue for government schools (payments have no relationship to having kids in school), and replace with tuition, 3) Terminate the federal 'No Child Left Behind' program as too costly, mostly counterproductive, and
an unconstitutional violation of states rights, 4) Eliminate the federal Dept. of Education, and 5) Write tax laws that encourage donors to create scholarships and endowments to provide affordable access to these private nonprofit schools for needy students. All these changes will allow parents to choose the school that best fits their children's needs (including religion) instead of pouring more tax dollars into the

present failing system. 'Do-gooders' will complain that the above approach does not guarantee a certain level (to 9th or 12th grade?) for every child due to negligent or poor parents. They prefer equal mediocrity for all. However, history shows that incentive, parents, and liberty produce much better results than government schools, while private charity helps those in need.

16. Environment

It is important to not cause excess pollution, erosion, floods, noise, odors, or other changes to the natural state that creates hazards or violate property rights, or threats thereto. Remember, your property not only includes land, buildings, cars, etc., but also your body, thus health hazards are included.

My position: Most problems can be handled from a property rights perspective by suing the source for restitution (not just a fine paid to the government). For example, toxic smoke, underground or surface liquid toxics that enter your body, land or other property can be litigated as property damage. Nuisance items such as odors and noise that come upon your property are the same. For non-owned items such as wild animals, protective legislation can be passed, but it is important to not violate other property and personal rights (such as farmers) in the process.

17. Immigration, and Border Security: Problems: Having a 'Work Permit' (green card), becoming a 'permanent resident' or citizen of the US is a privilege that should include a set of rules and obligations. You must apply, be accepted, and follow the rules, or don't come. Our country was built by immigrants who came here to work, be free, adopt the USA as their new homeland, and become Americans (use our language and laws), and that is still desirable. But now, in addition to jobs and freedom, free health, education and other benefits are part of the attraction, and most immigrants (legal and illegal) have no intention of assimilating as Americans. Many citizens, legislators, and foreign governments, want to use immigration as a 'social refuge system' which allows the poor and displaced of other nations to come here and be taken care of (welfare, etc.), rather than work to cure the problems in their homeland. Thus, the Federal government deposits hundreds of Somalis, Hmong, Russian Jews, etc. in communities, without permission of the State government or community. More federal unfunded mandates, arrogance and loss of States Rights! Thus the US has become a 'salad bowl' instead of a 'melting pot' and many immigrants become a burden on our benefits system. They often replace citizens working in low-paying jobs, adding to welfare costs and cultural stress, especially for blacks. Many unskilled citizens have lost their jobs to illegal immigrants. The 'illegal aliens' (a term often replaced by 'undocumented', as if they are victims or otherwise legal) are a further risk because they bypass checks on health and criminal records.

Illegal aliens take advantage of our freedoms by getting bolder and publicly demanding 'immigrant rights' (in-state tuition to college, health/welfare benefits, free K-12 school, etc.) even though they are trespassers in our land. The Mar-2006 mass demonstrations in many US cities are a good example. They were timed to occur a week before Congress started debate on new laws.

Minimum wage laws are a big part of this problem. Most laws require pay of $7 per hour or more, and many jobs don't justify this pay (i.e., employer can't make a profit), so employers look for other solutions. Cheap immigration labor is one alternative because they will work for cash at under $7 hour (this saves FICA payment for the employer also). It is said that Americans won't take the below minimum wage jobs, so immigrants are needed in order to get unskilled work done. WRONG! Americans will do the work, but wage laws prevent them being offered at low rates. If the competitive market doesn't support the prices needed to cover the high minimum wage, the jobs disappear, or are secretly given to illegals. When displaced by cheap illegal immigrant workers, our unskilled citizens may just go on welfare, leading to cultural problems and higher government expenses. Illegal immigration is not the answer to achieving price reductions! Most politicians ignore illegal immigration because: 1) cheap labor is sought by their campaign donors, or 2) immigrants are likely to vote for politicians who hand out the free services (in most states it is easy to just get the ID needed to register from a trash bin). Illegal immigration is increasing because of: 1) the ease of walking over the border, 2) the corruption and restrictions that inhibit creation of jobs in their homeland, and 3) lax enforcement by the INS at the border and in the US.

The government of Mexico lobbies against US immigration reform because it wants the $20 billion dollars per year their people in the US send home (known as 'remittances'). After oil, this repatriated money is the second biggest source of income for Mexico.

The Mexican government also encourages illegal immigration because it relieves pressure to reform the government socialism and corruption that reduces job creation in Mexico. Their Ambassador refuses to use the term 'illegal' in reference to those who sneak over the border when interviewed on TV, and they published a booklet to assist illegal entry.

Few people know that Mexico has many restrictions on Americans who live there. Americans cannot own property, or get citizen-style health and education benefits, such as they demand here. While the Mexican government not only requests, but claims special rights for 'their people' in the U.S., it is a FELONY to be an illegal immigrant in Mexico, subject to fines, imprisonment and deportation. What dishonesty and chutzpa !! What a bizarre one-way deal they are demanding!!

Our proud and historic tradition as a 'melting pot' is being abused. There are lumps and islands in the pot made of people who are here illegally, or refuse to assimilate.

My Solution: 1) Employers should be required to verify legal status of all current employees and then all new hires, of any ethnic group (hence, there would be no charges of profiling), and have the government ship the illegal persons home. Once the word is out that deporting is being done, many would leave on their own. A problem is that in most cases the origin country will not allow them to return!! This blockagemust be ended by negotiation.
2) Border restrictions, and temporary resident permits, should be enforced. Laws against harboring criminals and abetting illegal acts should be enforced. This means 'no sanctuary cities'! This will stop the work of bleeding-heart liberals and misguided religious folks from encouraging and performing illegal acts.
3) The 14 th Amendment should be revised or interpreted, so 'birthright citizenship' does not apply to children of illegal aliens. Since the loosened rules in the Immigration Act of 1965 a flood of immigrants, then their relatives, have come to the US primarily for jobs, and benefits, and most have no intention of learning English or assimilating (i.e., becoming 'Americans').
4) Proficiency in English should be a requirement for citizenship. The U.S. should adopt English as an official language for all government documents and discussions, including voting info. This will reduce costs, and encourage

assimilation. Having public documents (by both business and government) issued in multiple languages, and so-called 'multiculturalism', creates a trend toward cultural disintegration in any country. The 2006 riots in France, Germany, Australia, and England are examples of the results.

5) Immigrants must agree to follow U.S. laws. If you want to live under Islamic 'Sharia', don't come! Religious activity, such as Islamic calls to prayer on loudspeakers which cover a neighborhood, must be treated as a violation of the neighbor's property rights.

6) The concept of 'hyphenated Americans' (such as 'Mexican-, and African-American') should be discouraged (but not made illegal), since it tends to slow assimilation and create separate sub-cultures. This hyphenation is a sign of resistance to assimilation (a desire to keep your group separate). There should be an oath (spoken, written, witnessed, and signed) upon becoming a citizen that the person will adopt the USA as their new homeland, and give it their first loyalty above their religion and former homeland.

7) Enforce the fact that illegal immigrants have no 'rights' except humane treatment while they are being deported!

In March-2006 there were huge demonstrations in many U.S. cities by immigrants (legal and illegal) demanding there self-made 'rights' that they claim are about the same as U.S. citizens!

One of the best solutions is to improve the legal immigration process. Excessive delays (years), and rude staff (both are typical problems in government programs), cause many otherwise honest immigrants to sneak in.

18. Private Property and Eminent Domain: Private property rights are the foundation of a just and prosperous nation. History, and the world today, shows that justice and prosperity are reduced by lack of such rights. 'Partial Takings' abound due to down-zoning of property by the government at all levels (Federal to city). An example is when they rule that, to maintain 'open space', a farmer can't lease a patch of his ground along a road to a billboard firm. At the very least, he should be compensated for loss of income, and land value. The examples are legion. If the 'community' wants open-space, let them pay for it! The same logic applies for abuse of eminent domain, where 'public use' is applied to taking (owner is forced to sell at an appraised price) someone's home so a business that sells to the 'public' can use the land for a store, condos, etc. Liberals like to take money from 'the rich' using 'gang theft by vote' to fund their projects, so it is only a small step to use eminent domain to take land! I will fight to stop this abuse.

19. Gun Ownership

Activist groups have attempted to limit private gun ownership by citing the threat of accidents in the home and killings (single or mass) by crazed or criminal people. They attempt to eliminate damage by deviates and criminals by restricting everyone. The Dec-2012 Newton, CT killings prompted Pres. Obama and other to seek prohibition, and other restrictions, on a long list of guns.

My Position: The second amendment to the Constitution is usually cited as the legal basis to own a gun, but this is related to state militias (why else mention it). In fact, gun ownership is an inherent right, the same as owning a potentially lethal device such as a car, knife or ball bat, and it is only improper use that should be subject to public concern or government regulation. Concern over gun abuse is more emotional than real. The record shows that most gun-owners are very safety conscious. Since the 1930s the population has more than doubled, the number of guns in the US has quintupled, yet firearm accidents have been cut in half. A 2002 study in Maryland shows firearms average 0.8% of unintentional deaths in over the 18-year span. As to hazards to children in the home and family life, drownings take more lives of children under 14 than firearms by a factor of 18 over the period. Even knives, bees, and scissors take more children's lives than firearms. More children suffocate (e.g., choke on solid food) by a factor of 16 than die from firearms. As to killings by criminals, the government's war on drugs has created drug dealer turf wars that account for over 90% of deaths by guns in the U.S. These killers can get guns no matter what restrictions are put on purchases!

In some cases in the last ten years, the crazed killer may have been affected by medicines that control depression, anxiety, etc., as discussed in this link **http://lewrockwell.com/rappoport/rappoport13.1.html** . Another stimulant may be to copy the immoral and illegal 'justified' killings that our government does when they invade nations for political (control) and economic (oil, etc.) reasons. Killing becomes viewed as 'normal' and 'routine'. All the above issues and facts are ignored by the gun grabbers! In England, Canada, and Australia where gun ownership is highly restricted, burglaries and muggings (even daylight home robberies) have increased because criminals feel safe. The deterrent effect that your target person may have a gun is gone. In states where concealed-carry is allowed, muggings and armed-robberies decrease because criminals are afraid their targets may be armed. The same applies to schools where the principal or a guard may be armed. I say activists should focus on real threats and leave responsible gun owners alone.

An unstated, but key, reason to restrict gun ownership is the governments' desire to disarm the people so they can't defend themselves when the government raids their home, arrests without warrant, etc.

20. Social Programs; Welfare and Culture: **Our vast social programs, preferred minorities, and uncontrolled**

immigration, are destroying our culture. We are at the 'tipping point' in many areas where benefit recipients and new (often illegal) immigrants control the vote. Government has become Mother and Boss, and people become dependent and demand handouts and other special treatment as 'rights', rather than working for their own success. Ethics are in decline because one's reputation matters less when a person is shielded by Mother's laws. Law breaking and misconduct thrive.

I want all levels of government to 'back off' and let people manage their own affairs and interaction. Private welfare and counseling (such as Red Cross, Salvation Army, Goodwill, churches, private orgs, etc.) will serve the truly needy well. Further, private groups require less than half as much money to do the job due to better efficiency, and reduced overhead, fraud and abuse. The end of the 'entitlement' attitude and laws will cause people to manage their lives better. There will be fewer self-made 'victims', and more 'responsible citizens'. Incentives rule !!

Humans thrive in an environment where they are comfortable with the region's personal value system, laws, religious attitudes, etc. This gives the feeling of 'home'. A common language has a lot to do with this bonding.

Today, a high percentage of immigrants (legal and illegal) have no intention of assimilating. They are only here for jobs and benefits. This will lead to strife for all.

History and logic show that my 'less government intervention' approach not only yields more liberty, but more peace, justice, prosperity and better ethics. This approach rewards personal responsibility and work, and private charity cares well for the needy (and there are about 80% fewer cases due to reduced abuse, reduced perverse incentives-i.e., 'career' welfare users-, lower costs due to use of volunteers, and no 'entitlements').

The 'more government' systems, such as pushed by Progressives, Liberals, and Socialists, have the opposite effect, and do more harm than good (counting side-effects)

When people become dependent on government, they care less about support from, and relationships with, friends and family. As these relationships whither, other social problems such as crime, broken homes, and laziness grow.

21. Gay, Ethnic, and Hate Laws
There are many conflicts in the law as to what gays (homosexual persons) can do. Marriage and adoption are active now. Most churches view gay conduct as a sin (i.e., wrong even if you are not violating or threatening another's rights; see issue 2, 'Core Principle' above). Of course, those who consider it a sin (or on any subject; abortion, gambling, etc.) are free to peacefully promote their views, short of violating the rights of the so-called 'sinners', by ;1) Setting an example by their conduct, and 2) Lobbying the government for passage of laws to impose their views on others by force.

I view these conflicts as examples of why the government should 'back off' and abolish laws that control our lives by favors and restrictions (i.e., social engineering). Marriage is a personal matter and none of the government's business. Favorable tax laws for married persons should be abolished. A 'marriage contract' will handle inheritance, etc., and should be used by all; gay and straight. Adoption should be controlled by the birth parents and private orgs (if parents died together, gave-up rights, etc.).

Laws giving any group special rights and preferential treatment (which creates a 'preferred minority') should be abolished also. Such laws are easily abused by ethnic persons or groups. For example, 1. In Oct-2007, the former football coach of a major U.S. university won a $2 million judgment claiming the school fired him because of his race (black), not his 6-27 won-loss record, and 2. A minority person now feels free to park illegally (including at the front door!) of a shopping center, or post office, etc., since usually no one will challenge them for fear of a lawsuit, or being attacked! 'Hate Crime' laws are another example. There should be no 'special' penalties; murder is murder. All citizens should have the same rights, with no special rights or privileges for gays, or any other group, as to race, sex, economic or social status, religion, etc. (see 'Core Principle' in Issue # 2 above). People should be able to associate with (or avoid) whomever they want without fear of lawsuit for violation of special 'civil rights', and the same applies to clubs, employers, etc. as to membership, hiring, and firing (short of violating a person's legal rights). This approach leads to a just and harmonious society, where people learn to 'get along' without government coercion.

Restrictions and favors do more harm than good as to improving social, and economic success of minority groups. Special rights and subsidies reduce incentive for self-improvement, and create the opportunity to abuse such rights. Intrusion in people's lives is unconstitutional and none of the government's business.

22. The Drug War : Our legal system for drugs is antiquated and distorted with hypocrisy and inconsistencies. 'Drugs' such as nicotine and caffeine (stimulants, uppers) and alcohol (a depressant, downer) are legal to use and available anywhere. They are both damaging to health, but are legal for political reasons (voter demand, campaign contributions)), and because the government wants the tax revenue. Other uppers and downers are illegal. Extracts of marijuana with proven medicinal uses are illegal, while morphine (made from otherwise illegal opium) is used by doctors for pain suppression. Why is one OK and not the other? Changes are needed. While excess use of 'sporting' drugs is a serious medical and social problem, only fools and ignorant youths do it. However, I say criminalization of such stupid activity only makes it worse (our experience with alcohol prohibition is a good comparison). Further, such use is none of the government's business unless the user violates or threatens someone else's rights (see Dave's 'Core Principle' in issue # 2 above). The FDA and our 'War on Drugs' do much more harm than good. Users can get drugs easily even after years of the Drug War (but they cost more now), and the violent 'turf wars' of pushers and gangs, plus burglaries and muggings by users to support their habit, are worse than ever. It also corrupts police; 1) With the easy abuse of 'asset forfeiture' laws. They can be imposed as 'civil' arrests on just 'suspects'; no profit on illegal acts; they can confiscate – and own – any asset that was 'associated' with a 'suspected' crime. This includes local police taking title to, and selling (their department keeps the money!), cars, boats, planes, ranches, etc. without trial. The owner can sue for return, but this takes time and money and may not work, and 2) By the funding and excitement from SWAT Team 'combat' style attitudes and raiding equipment. My solution is to treat drugs like alcohol and nicotine (tax it and control age of buyer and offer optional control on purity of product), and handle abusers as; a) A mental and medical problem, or b) Illegal if a user threatens others, such as driving a car while high. Abuse and violence will soon subside, just as with alcohol, after the end of prohibition. The fact that many drugs are more potent than alcohol makes it even more urgent to get such business out of the hands of criminals.

23. Energy: Problem: Energy costs and consumption are going up worldwide, while oil reserves and production (barrels per day, B/D) are going down. The world's daily production averaged 83 million B/D in 2004, and the USA consumed about 25% of it (with only 4% of the world's population). Production of 'cheap oil' (cheap to find, pump and refine) is forecast to decline to 39 mill. B/D by 2030 while consumption increases to 118 ! This is the 'peak oil' concept, where wells in liquid oil pools start to produce less per day. The difference will have to be made up by coal, natural gas, tar-sands, shale-oil (by 'fracking'), nuclear, wind, solar, and bio-fuel, algae farms, etc., plus reduced consumption and more CONSERVATION !! Each fuel has its own economic, technical, and enviro issues. Oil has been cheap to get, and convenient to use, so has been the first choice so far. As the price of oil goes up, these alternate fuels will become more attractive, especially if renewable and/or sustainable. Consumption by China and India is growing faster than any other country. They are shopping for long-term OIL DEALS, big time! This ties-in with why Bush invaded Afghanistan and Iraq, and Obama is threatening Iran (as I write in Jan-2013); namely to control the Greater Mid East oil producers (including Uzbekistan, other 'xxstans', the Caspian area, and North Africa) before other countries make deals for it. An underlyimg reason is to prevent access by China, thus limiting their growth. USA leaders want it ALL! Solution: I recommend; 1. End the Afghanistan and Iraq wars, and engage in peaceful oil-supply negotiations with all producers worldwide (we are a big customer, and they need us!), 2. Allow eco-friendly oil drilling in all parts of the USA. Note that the Audubon Society has done this in their preserves, 3. Encourage development of alternate fuels and methods (such as electricity from new-generation engines, solar, hydro and nuclear, but no subsidies), and 4. Allow gas and oil prices to rise to their free-market levels, without subsidies or control, but with appropriate anti-pollution laws based on property-rights (of your body, water, air, and land) for those people and places at present or future risk. The past errors, distortions and fears of nuclear energy need to be updated and corrected so the new and safe methods for generation of electricity can be employed. Safer thorium could replace uranium. These four changes will give incentive for conservation and production of alternate energy. The free market is very good at responding to demand. Government bureaucrats always spend more and accomplish less than people using their own money, and their projects usually do more harm than good. For example, consider the politically-driven scandal of subsidies for ethanol, which is toxic, expensive, causes land misuse by excess corn production, is bad for the environment, and increases food prices, etc. BOO ! Algea farms, using flooded ponds, have good potential because they; use minimal fertilizer; can use areas with bad soil; and can use saltwater. New 'external combustion' engines are more efficient, and can burn low grade fuels. For a comprehensive list of energy choices, see **www.peswiki.com**.

24. Traits of Capitalism and Corporations: Liberals, Socialists, and Progressives like to attack 'Capitalism' and label it as a 'social system', and 'corporations' as bastions of greed and abuse. However, Capitalism is properly defined in my 1953 and 1961 dictionaries as an 'economic system' based on private ownership and free enterprise. It is also a moral system because all conduct is voluntary. Current dictionaries have crept toward defining it as a 'social system' as Liberal editors take control; very convenient, but false. A Corporation is just a legal structure to allow shared ownership and financing. Liberals like to say that corps are a way to avoid personal responsibility. These definitions were invented by Liberals as straw men to avoid their own complicity in corrupt and unconstitutional government.

It is bad 'people' (as usual; same for churches and governments), bad laws, corrupt government (including legal 'favors', subsidies, etc.), and perverse incentives that cause the trouble. Liberals avoid criticizing government because they want it to keep giving the legal favors and welfare, but only to their projects. What a pile of ignorance and hypocrisy! For example, the June 26, 2002 main editorial in the Wall Street Journal, by Dr. Henry Manne (George Mason Univ., Univ. of Chicago, etc.), made a great point that the Williams Act of 1968 (now rules 13d and 14d of the 1934 Securities Act) was the birth of the Boardroom and Officer fraud and self-dealing we have been seeing since the '80s (it took a few years to set in). The new law required takeover groups to announce their intent once they had 5 % of the target stock, which gave warning so officers could protect themselves. This allowed officers of many firms to get lazy and corrupt without risk of getting booted-out. Remember, corporations become takeover targets only because their profits, and return on assets, are low, usually due to bad management. In takeovers, the shareholders win, but bad managers lose! Thus, at-risk bad managers whine to the government for protection (can you say 'campaign donation'?). Many states have passed laws to 'protect' their local firms from 'outsiders', and the 'poison pill' was born to fend-off the takeover groups! Another factor is the shareholder laziness that developed in the 1990s as stock prices soared due to inflation. The attitude was 'all's well', 'no worries'. It wasn't long (and quite predictable) that the nomination of Directors by shareholders was restricted, and biased 'Buddy' Directors were selected by Officers (a 'slate'). The self-dealing started, and the combined 'Chairman and CEO' position was born (an inherent conflict) ! These hot-shot CEOs plundered their firms with huge salaries and stock options, while trying to set a glorious, resume-enhancing, growth record with short-term, unsustainable, profit enhancements (reduce staff, announce grand plans, etc.), and excess debt, spending and risk They often got themselves and their firms in business or legal trouble, but left with 'golden handshakes' or hung around a while with 'retention bonuses'.

There are hundreds of examples! Why should a low-performing, or corrupt, CEO get a multi-million dollar bonus when fired?? It is white-collar theft! The Dodd-Frank bill of July-2010 issued a vast set of rules to correct abuses, but puts a major compliance burden on firms.
Solution: I say the solution is to repeal the Williams Act, and other distortions of the free market, not pass a slew of new regulations. Let the free market do its work, so shareholders will wake-up then nominate and vote for honest, competent Directors that select and monitor the officers.

25. Origins of 2008 Crash and Effect of Bailouts

The rush of home loan defaults and bank problems started in late 2007, and peaked in Sep-2008, and is continuing, but less, at this writing in Jan-2013. The underlying cause was Fake Money, as described in Chapter 3. This excess supply of money, delivered to lenders by the Fed and its pals at FreddieMac and FannieMae, was the 'mother's milk' of market distortion. A trigger was the 4.25% increase (from 1% to 5,25%) in interest set by Greenspan when he ended his Fed term in Jan-2006.

A major facilitator was the Community Reinvestment Act (CRA), a 1977 federal law that requires **banks** and **thrifts** to offer **credit** throughout their entire market area and prohibits them from targeting only wealthier neighborhoods with their services, a practice known as "**redlining**." The purpose of the CRA is to provide (force?) credit, including home ownership opportunities, to 'underserved' (unqualified?) populations and commercial loans to small businesses. OK, getting their votes may be part of it!

The CRA was passed into law by the U.S. Congress in 1977 as a result of national **grassroots** pressure for affordable housing, and despite considerable opposition from the mainstream banking community. The CRA mandates that each banking institution be evaluated to determine if it has met the credit needs of its entire community. In 1995, as a result of interest from President Clinton's administration, the implementing regulations for the CRA were strengthened by focusing the financial regulators' attention on institutions' performance in helping to meet community credit needs. These changes were very controversial and as a result, the regulators agreed to revisit the rule after it had been fully implemented for five years. Thus in 2002, the regulators opened up the regulation for review and potential revision.

The **Clinton** Administration's regulatory revisions with an effective starting date of **January 31**, **1995** were credited with substantially increasing the number and aggregate amount of loans to small businesses and to low- and moderate-income borrowers for home loans. Part of the increase in home loans was due to increased efficiency and the genesis of lenders, like **Countrywide** (set up as an 'off brand' by Bank of America), that was aggressive and did not mitigate loan risk with savings deposits (ie, borrowers must have deposits) as did traditional banks using the new subprime authorization. This is known as the secondary market for mortgage loans (high risk for banks). The revisions allowed the **securitization** (packaging, with insurance, and called AAA; FRAUD!!) of CRA loans containing **subprime mortgages**. The first public **securitization** of CRA loans started in 1997 by **Bear Stearns**, and it helped break them in Sep-2008!. The number of CRA mortgage loans increased by 39 percent between 1993 and 1998, while other loans increased by only 17 percent (a flood of money into high risk).

In the 1980s, groups such as the activists at ACORN ('Association of Community Organizations for Reform Now', **www.acorn.org**; an Obama favorite!) began pushing charges of "redlining" - claims that banks discriminated against minorities in mortgage lending. In 1989, sympathetic members of Congress got the Home Mortgage Disclosure Act amended to force banks to collect racial data on mortgage applicants; this allowed various studies to be ginned up that seemed to validate the original accusation.

In fact, minority mortgage applications were rejected more frequently than other applications - but the overwhelming reason wasn't racial discrimination, but simply that minorities tend to have weaker finances. A study in 1992 proved that bias was not the problem. Yet the harm was done and banks loosened their rules to avoid lawsuits.

A good example is an article on the government's takeover of Chrysler as written by Peter Schiff (see P. 207, #18) on May 5, 2009 and quoted in part here: "…A real bankruptcy is the only solution. In it, current shareholders get wiped out, current contracts and obligations are voided, which creates the opportunity for new management, with private capital, to scrap out-of-date business practices, and produce cars cheaply and profitably. Under the guise of 'saving jobs', the Administration has disrupted this process."

Illegally giving control of Chrysler and GM to the UAW and the government in 2009 enshrined a culture of failure and sealed Detroit's fate. Both companies have become government-sponsored entities, not too dissimilar from Amtrak or the Post Office, forever relying on taxpayer funds to create products of dubious quality." Sure enough, Detroit is now full of decay and crime. The police have given-up on serving some neighborhoods!

The statist approach of Obama's 'government intervention and control' will make the economic recovery worse and longer. His re-election in Nov-2012 adds to the potential amount of economic and cultural damage!

26. Occupational and Business Licenses:
Problem: Licenses are touted as a way to protect citizens from faulty or fraudulent services, but in fact usually limit choices to the citizens and give 'cartel or monopoly' status to the license holders. This applies to lawyers, doctors, plumbers,

beauticians, restaurants, contractors, etc. where the licensing is often abused by; 1. The government, and incumbent licensees, to restrict new entrants in order to protect themselves and friends from competition, and 2. By associations (unions, medical, legal, etc.) to impose rules such as minimum fees to clients, controlled or no advertising of rates, etc. The government has threatened cancellation of a license to force 'cooperation', such as making phone companies give them private usage data, or radio and TV treat them 'nice'. Another category is when the citizen is subject to, or can be threatened by, the service provider without initiating choice. An example is a truck driver or airline pilot, where one can be run into, or be in a crash, if an unqualified person is providing the service. These should be licensed to PROTECT the citizen, a proper function of government.

Solution: I recommend that licenses be optional when the citizen can initiate choice of the service provider. This would; 1. Allow individuals and firms to offer services, and set and advertise prices, without permission from the government or a 'professional society' or union (let the buyer beware, and decide), 2. Allow groups to form 'professional societies' or unions that set their own standards of quality, disclosure of member skills and performance records, and membership requirements, and advertise them, without government control, and 3. Bring the benefits of competition (better quality, lower prices) to the trade groups (yes, doctors and lawyers are a trade group).

Buyers who prefer a government-licensed provider, could use one; but all buyers (patients, clients, etc.) would have a CHOICE of licensed or unlicensed. Of course, it follows that the chooser would be responsible for the results and could not sue a vendor for being incompetent if unlicensed.

27. Limits on Terms and Benefits for Congress:

Problem: One cause of corruption in DC is that officials will do almost anything to keep their prestigious and profitable jobs (pork to voters; favors to campaign donors, etc.). Furthermore, they vote themselves pension, health and other benefits that far exceed what they bestow on their constituents. Examples are; a) Better pensions and health care than Social Security and Medicare, b) Their children can include student loan debt in a bankruptcy, c) Any campaign funds existing when they retire belongs to them. Can you say 'Privileged Upper Class'?

Solution: I recommend that: 1. No U.S. Representative may serve more than four terms (8 years), two terms (12 years) for a Senator, or a combined fourteen years if they have worked in both jobs (based on a combined life total), 2. All elected officials get the same pension (Social Security) and health (Medicare) benefits as the 'common' citizens, and with the same rules for calculating fees, and reimbursement of claims, and 3. End any other special treatment that is found.

28. Eliminate 'Earmark' Pork Funding:
Most Congresspersons like to 'bring home the pork' to fund
state projects and win votes. These 'earmarks' are hidden,
unconstitutional, add-ons to other funding bills such as
transportation, and 'Omnibus Appropriations Bills' (5 or
10 funding bills combined), and are not discussed in the
normal approval process, yet add-up to billions of dollars per
year. Even worse, the omnibus bills are usually many
hundreds of pages and few Congresspersons read any part
of them! Since the government is already 'in the red', this
spending is a serious add-on to our national debt problem! I
will promote a bill to make earmarks and Omnibus
Appropriation Bills (and sneaky 'Minibus' bills) illegal for all
Congresspersons. This will eliminate cries by some voters of;
'We're not getting our share of pork'. Of course we will also
fight for reductions and elimination of improper grants and
subsidies. Unfortunately, in May-2009, Pres. Obama blessed
earmarks by saying; 'The local Congressperson knows best
what his/her District needs.' Another campaign pledge
trashed!

29. Nullification of Federal Laws by States: In general,
nullification is refusal to enforce a law deemed unconstitutional
or otherwise illegal. It originates in the concern of government
becoming too strong or abusive, and ignoring the Constitution
and laws. Key applications are;

1) Refusal of States to enforce Federal laws; State
sovereignty over the Federal government is the basis. Recent
examples are state nullifications of all, or portions of, the
REAL ID Act of 2005, medical marijuana laws, Cap and Trade,
and the Second Amendment restrictions

2) Refusal of a jury to enforce charges imposed by a law or the court; **This** relates to sovereignty of the citizens over all levels of government. On this basis, juries can refuse to impose the penalties decided upon by the court. Over the years, judges and lawyers have made it illegal, confirming the original concern; They want more power!

My position is that nullification is necessary as a check on excess and immoral use of power by the government. Tom Woods Ph.D. explains it well in his book; *'NULLIFICATION: HOW TO RESIST FEDERAL TYRANNY IN THE 21ST CENTURY'.*

30. Secession by States from the USA: The USA was created by secession of the colonies from England. The new 'states' were sovereign entities that created a Federal government, limited in scope by a Constitution. It was a voluntary association that could be ended by the members.

Early examples of 'creeping federal dominance' that violate our freedoms and States Rights were: 1) The Civil War (actually a war of aggression by the North; the South just wanted to leave, not take-over the government) established the Federal government as superior in power to the States based on 'might-is-right', and 2) The Pledge of Allegiance, written in 1892 by Francis Bellamy (a socialist Baptist minister who was fired for his socialist sermons) which included the word 'indivisible'. In 1954, Congress after a campaign by the catholic Knights of Columbus, added the words, 'under God', making the Pledge both a patriotic oath and a public prayer. Both terms are improper because; a) our allegiance should be to the nation (the land and people), not the government, and b) 'under God' violates separation of church and state (inserting religion into a text, place, etc. that is used, and owned, by all).Recent Federal mandates (Obama's health care, 'No Child Left Behind', TSA, drug laws, etc., etc.) have awakened interest in secession because they violate the Constitution. States Rights, and our fundamental rights of self-government, and voluntary association. Groups in many

States have sent secession petitions to the White House! Secession is a proper reaction to abusive and illegal acts by the federal government. As a first step, secession petitions can be a tool to alert Congress and the President to the need for changes. Opponents cite the Article 6 'Supremacy Clause' in the Constitution (which can be argued only applies to laws that are Constitutional). The Swiss use their Referendum process to change laws and terminate the jobs of politicians. We should do the same. In the absence of corrections from DC, full secession can be employed (similar to referendum in #31 below).

31. Constitutional Amendments: a. Referendum Laws

: The Swiss have been very successful in controlling government abuses and excesses by use of their referendum laws which allow them to; 1) Remove legislators from office (recall), 2) Pass laws that they want but can't get the self-serving legislators to pass, and 3) Repeal laws that they don't like. This keeps the legislators alert to comply with the voter's wishes, and gives voters incentive to be active in managing their country (rather than whining as 'victims'). It is close to 'direct democracy'. I suggest a similar set of rules be invoked in the USA, and

b. A Balanced Budget amendment will give us a powerful tool to limit spending. Politicians will like it because they can claim; 'We want to give you more, but our hands are tied!'

32. Abortion : Problem: There will always be abortions. The legality and conditions are what vary. Roe v Wade, and government payments in many cases, have made abortion so cheap and convenient it is often treated as a means of contraception. Carelessness and irresponsibility are rampant. Solution: I am personally opposed to abortion except to protect the mother's life, and say in no case should the government pay the costs. I further oppose abortion after the first trimester (3 months is plenty of time to make up your mind), and all partial-birth abortions (except for major malformation of the fetus). However, one should not seek laws

to force others to comply with one's own value system. Again, The 'Core Principle' applies (see Item 1b above). The question is. 'When does the fetus become a separate person with rights?' Many people take the position that abortion is a moral or religious issue, and assert that 'life begins upon conception' and the fetus is an 'unborn child', just as they righteously assert their dogma about deities, angels, virgin births, Heaven, Hell, etc. in the absence of supporting logic or fact. These are sincere positions, but do not negate the fact that the fetus is not a separate person with rights until born. It is a living part of the mother's body, like her arm, but not a 'person' with rights.

As to the law, a woman's body is her property, and does not belong to the government, her doctor, or her church. Thus, it is a woman's right to make an informed choice on what happens to her body. In fact, for a responsible woman there are a series of three choices involved. Whether to;
1) Have sex, 2) Use protection, and if pregnant,
3) Deliver a baby, or have an abortion.
The Roe vs Wade ruling is invalid because the Federal government has no constitutional authority in this area. Thus it is a State issue. **In summary**:

1. Opponents of abortion should not attempt to impose their personal views or religious beliefs on others by force of law. That would be immoral and unconstitutional. They should peacefully oppose abortion without using force or threat to the pregnant woman, or her doctors and staff and their facilities.
2. Proponents should exercise their right without expecting others (including via the government) to pay for it, and they should observe the three choices above.

33. End of Life Choices: Modern technology allows terminally ill people to live longer, but usually at great expense and suffering (a socially mandated form of torture). To avoid this harm, our laws and societal standards need to be revised as follows. Current law gives four choices for the patient and family; 1. Increasing pain medication (for comfort), 2. Terminal sedation (keep the patient completely unconscious until death occurs), 3. Withdrawing treatments and life-support, and 4. Advance authorization to doctors and family filed by the patient while healthy as a 'living will' and/or 'power of attorney'. Self-inflicted, and patient-approved 'assisted suicide' are illegal (remember Dr. Kervorkian?), but this ignores that in a free society you own your life and body (the government and church don't). It is none of the government's business what you do to yourself, thus should be legal. 'Mercy killing' (no patient approval), is illegal due to possible misuse, but should be made legal with adequate controls (such as family approval when available; always a medical statement that the subjects' comatose is incurable). Moral and religious issues are optional personal choices. Note that the above changes do not grant any legal authority to the government. It is all about personal Liberty.

****

Summary: I hope you have found my writings in Part 1

above interesting and useful. I now offer the additional references and sources of info in Part 2 below. Thank you for your interest in learning about, and hopefully working to solve, the problems discussed in this book.

As also proposed on p. 12, please help **Restore the USA** by working to start the Movement and Revolution!

First, please join our 'Forward USA Club', by sending me your email address to my address below, and I will put you on the Club newsletter list so we can coordinate our work. I will serve as President of the Club.

The Home page of my blog www.SaferInvesting.org has news about the **'Forward USA Club'**. A newsletter, including financial information, will be sent to members monthly.

I need your financial help to cover the cost of printing and sending this book to 'leaders' nationwide, and for other activities to promote the club and achieve our goals. Please send your check (not tax deductible), payable to **'Forward USA',** to PO Box 8432, Madison, WI 53708. Please include return contact info (email is fine). I will deposit all funds in our account at UW Credit Union, Madison, WI. An annual donation of $25 is suggested, which includes a 'Restore..' book. The Clubs' monthly newsletter will document all income and expenses.

My authors' cost for the book is about $4, plus about $ 5 for shipping (in to me and out –with a letter- to a 'leader'). An updated book will be sent each year (to refresh their brains) to the President, all Congresspersons and Senators, Governors, Judges, Agency Heads, key staff persons, and candidates. Other 'urgent topic' letters will be mailed, and I will seek appearances as a radio, TV, or seminar speaker, guest, or panel member. Funds are used only for Club expenses. I receive no pay; just expenses. **Thanks**

If you have questions or suggestions, please contact me at **RedickD@aol.com**.

Thanks and Best regards, Dave Redick

Part 2
Contents:

****

#1. References & Info Sources

Contents: A. Authors- P. 202, B. Books- P. 208
C. Org. and Internet Info Sites- P. 210

A. Authors

1. Pat Buchanan: In his book **'Day of Reckoning**: How Hubris, Ideology, and Greed Are Tearing America Apart", 2006, Pat says that America is facing a crisis from which it may not survive. He argues that the effects of mass immigration, ineffective foreign policy, and an overextended military, are leading the country on a path of destruction. Pat has written eleven books including; **'The Unnecessary War'**, **'A Republic Not An Empire'**, **'The Death of the West'**, and **'Suicide of a Superpower'**, 2011. More at his blog **www.Buchanan.org**.

2. Douglas R. Casey: In his book **'Crisis Investing'**, 1979, Doug predicted a major depression due to government intervention. It came in 2008! He; 1) Is an independent thinker, with 'on the ground' business experience (not biased by academic rules and vanity), 2) Supports liberty, the gold standard, and limited government as the path to peace and prosperity, and 3) Writes books about investing and government; His book **'TOTALLY INCORRECT"**, 2012, with L. James and T. Coxon, is an unabashed treatise for libertarianism and free-market capitalism; **'Crisis Investing'**, 1995; and **'The International Man'** 1979, with H. Schulz. His newest book 'Speculator'(Sep-2016) is his first novel, and first in a planned series of 7. See his articles: 1) Feb-2012 about war, oil, gov't, and gold at: **lewrockwell.com/casey/casey108**, 2) Mar-2012, 'The Ascendence of Sociopaths in US Governance' **lewrockwell.com/casey/casey112**, 3) Nov-2012 'The America That Was – Now the United (Police) State of America', **lewrockwell.com/casey/casey139, and**

4) http://lewrockwell.com/casey/casey150.html . His archives are at; lewrockwell.com/casey/casey-arch, and caseyresearch.com/cdd/archives.

3. **Thomas J. DiLorenzo Ph.D.** is the author of 'The Real Lincoln' **(Dec-2003),** 'Lincoln Unmasked' **(Nov-2007), and** 'How Capitalism Saved America'. **A professor of economics at Loyola College in Maryland and a senior fellow at the Ludwig von Mises Institute, he holds a** Ph.D. **in Economics from** Virginia Tech, **and has written for the Wall Street Journal, Barron's, and many other publications.**

4. Richard Ebeling, PhD.; Dr. Ebeling is the BB&T Distinguished Professor of Ethics and Free Enterprise Leadership at The Citadel (a university in Charleston, SC). He will be conducting courses such as "Leadership, Entrepreneurship, and Capitalist Ethics" as well as "The Morality and Economics of Capitalist Society." Dr. Ebeling is recognized as one of the leading members of the Austrian School of Economics and the author of 'POLITICAL ECONOMY, PUBLIC POLICY, AND MONETARY ECONOMICS: LUDWIG VON MISES AND THE AUSTRIAN TRADITION' (Routledge 2010. Visit **Citadel.edu**

5. Pepe Escobar is a Brazilian investigative journalist. He writes great articles about government treachery for **www.atimes.com**. He has focused on Central Asia and the Middle East since the late 1990s. and is the author of the books Globalistan: **How the Globalized World is Dissolving into Liquid War** (Jan-2007), **Obama Does Globalistan**, Jan-2009, and **Red Zone Blues'** Aug-2007. He invented the term 'pipelineistan' to cover the hidden political and shooting wars led by the U.S. to control the oil and gas in the Greater Mid East.

6. Stephen Greenhut is Vice President of Journalism at the Franklin Center for Government and Public Integrity (*FRANKLINCENTERHQ.ORG*). *HIS BOOKS ARE.* **'Plunder!, How Public Employee Unions are Raiding Treasuries…'** *in 2010 (SEE SEIU.ORG), AND **"ABUSE OF POWER: HOW THE GOVERNMENT MISUSES EMINENT DOMAIN"** IN 2004. SEE HIS ARTICLE;* **www.lewrockwell.com/greenhut/greenhut72.1** .

7. F. A. Hayek, Nobel Laureate. See; **'Denationalisation of Money: The Argument Refined'**, 1976, which puts forth the case to; 1) end the government monopoly on money creation, 2) let anyone create money, and 3) let the free market determine which type of money is used.

8. **Ron Holland** is an international retirement consultant, public speaker, stockbroker and author of three books (including 'Escape the Pension Trap') and numerous articles and special reports. He is a strong proponent of investment outside U.S. markets and the dollar as protection from America's exploding national debt. **More at:** thedailybell.com, www.RonHolland.com, www.bfi-consulting.com .

9. Laffer Ph.D., Arthur: While on the Reagan staff in the 1980s he was one of the creators of Supply-Side Economics and the Laffer Curve, which shows the tradeoff between tax rates and revenues. His books include '**End of Prosperity'**, and most recently '**Return to Prosperity'**. He earned an MBA and Ph.D. in economics from Stanford University. See more at www.laffercenter.com.

10. Eric Margolis wrote **'American Raj'**, 2008. He is an American with French and Canadian ties. His father was in the Foreign Service and he grew up in in the Mid East. As a long-time foreign correspondent for the Toronto Star, and others, he has traveled the world and has great insight about world events. See www.ericmargolis.com

11. Donald W. Miller, Jr., M.D. is a cardiac surgeon and Professor of Surgery at the University of Washington in Seattle. He is a member of **Doctors for Disaster Preparedness** and writes on politics, health and medicine. For a start, see his excellent '**A Fourteen Point Plan for a Post-Wilsonian America'** at **http://www.lewrockwell.com/orig2/miller2.html**, and his archives at **www.lewrockwell.com**. His web site is **www.donaldmiller.com**, which includes his CV and bio.

12. Gary K. North Ph.D. (born 1942) writes on economics, history, and theology. He received a **PhD** in history from the **University of California, Riverside** in 1972, and served as research assistant for **Congressman** Ron Paul **in 1976** His blogs are garynorth.com, and teapartyeconomist.com

13. Rep. Ron Paul M.D. (R, TX-14), wrote **'The Revolution: A Manifesto',** April 2008, and **'End the Fed'** in Sep-2009, and was a Republican candidate for President in 2008 and 2012. Dr. Paul says we have been lied to, robbed and used by our own government. Dr. Paul ended his last term as a Congressman in Jan-2013. On April 17, 2013 Dr. Paul announced creation of his '**Institute for Peace and Prosperity'**, with a mission to educate and advocate for a peaceful foreign policy and the protection of civil liberties at home (**ronpaulinstitute.org). Eric Margolis (# 10 above) and Butler Shaffer (# 18 below) are on his Academic Board.** See his archives at **http://www.lewrockwell.com/paul/paul-arch.html**, and his ongoing activity at CampaignforLiberty.org, and 'unofficial' news at ronpaul.com and dailypaul.com.

14. James Quinn, is Senior Director of Strategic Planning for a major university, and author of a series of essays on world financial affairs. See: 'WHAT HAPPENED TO THE AMERICAN DREAM', Dec. 24, 2008' at **http://www.financialsense.com/editorials/quinn/2008/12 24.html**, and 'The Law of Unintended Consequences: 20th

Century and Beyond' Jan. 5, 2009. For more, go to **http://seekingalpha.com/author/james-quinn** , www.financialsense.com/editorials/quinn/2009/0218, http://www.informationclearinghouse.info/article33527.html and his main site; **http://www.theburningplatform.com/** .

15. Paul Craig Roberts, Ph.D., is an economist and author of eight books and many articles on economics and politics; all non-PC, based on fact and logic, and seeking the truth. He; 1) Holds a Ph.D. from the **University of Virginia**, and was a post-graduate at the **University of California, Berkeley**, and **Oxford University** where he was a member of **Merton College**, 2) Worked for Rep. Jack Kemp and Pres. Reagan on the implementation of 'Supply-Side' economics (see P. 213), leading to his book **'The Supply-Side Revolution'** in 1984, 3) Is a former; a) Associate Editor of the Wall Street Journal, b) Contributing editor for National Review, and c) Assistant Secretary of the U.S. Treasury, and 4) Is the John M. Olin Fellow at the Institute for Political Economy and a Senior Research Fellow at the Hoover Institution, Stanford University. Other books (some co-authored) are; **'Capitalist Revolution in Latin America'**(1997), **'The Tyranny of Good Intentions'**(2008), **'How the Economy Was Lost'**(2010), and **'Failure of Laissez Faire Capitalism'**(6-2013), **How America was Lost'**, (3-2014), and **'The Neoconservative Threat to World Order'** (11-2015). His internet columns have attracted a worldwide following See his site **paulcraigroberts.org** (click 'Articles' for archives; including 'Assault on Gold'), and his full story at **en.wikipedia.org/wiki/Paul_Craig_Roberts**.

16. Murray Rothbard Ph.D., A great Austrian economist, Professor, and prolific author. See **'For a New Liberty'** and archives and books at **http://www.mises.org/money.asp**

17. Salerno, Joseph, PhD; Salerno is a professor of economics at **Pace University** (NY). He is the chair of the economics graduate program, and is also a senior faculty member of the **Mises Institute**, for which he frequently lectures and writes. He serves as editor of the Institute's **Quarterly Journal of Austrian Economics**.

18. Peter Schiff is President of Euro Pacific Capital and author of 'The Little Book of Bull Moves in Bear Markets' in 2008, 'Crash Proof: How to Profit from the Coming Economic Collapse' in 2007 (then a '2.0' version in 2011) and '**The Real Crash'** in 2012. All give 'real life' ideas for economics and investing. See his business site **http://www.europac.net/**, and archives at http://www.lewrockwell.com/schiff/schiff-arch.html

19. Butler Shaffer writes on the nature and threat of government and law in our lives. He holds both B.Sc. and B.A. degrees from the University of Nebraska, and a J.D. degree from the University of Chicago Law School. After practicing law for seven years, he is now a professor at Southwestern University School of Law in Los Angeles. His books are; 1. Violence as a Product of Imposed Order (1976), 2. In Restraint of Trade (1997, 2008), 3. Calculated Chaos (1985, 2004), 4. **Boundaries of Order** (2009), and 5. **The Wizards of Ozymandias** (2012). See **http://swlaw.edu/faculty/faculty_listing/facultybio/70115**

20. David Stockman was director of the Office of Management and Budget under President Ronald Reagan, serving from 1981 until August 1985. His Apr-2013 book "The Great Deformation: Corruption of Capitalism in America', discusses how central bank meddling and the breakdown of sound money have bludgeoned the free markets' capacity to generate wealth and growth. After leaving the government, he worked as an Investment Mgr. for Blackstone Grp., and then was a Founder and Director of www.heartlandpartners.com . He now publishes a newsletter 'Contra-Corner'. His latest book is '**Trumped'**, 9-2013, which warns how the USA faces economic and cultural failure due to excessive spending and taxation.

21. Robert Wenzel is editor and publisher of the 'Economic Policy Journal' (EconomicPolicyJournal.com) which provides a steady supply of free-market analysis on a broad range of topics.

22. Thomas E. Woods, Jr. Ph.D. holds a bachelor's degree in history from Harvard and his master's, M. Phil., and Ph.D. in history from Columbia University. He is the author of eleven books, most recently **ROLLBACK: REPEALING BIG GOVERNMENT BEFORE THE COMING FISCAL COLLAPSE**. More at **TomWoods.com**.

B. Books

1. **'Empire of Debt'**, a 2006 book by W. Bonner and A. Wiggins. It addresses how excessive national debt and spending can drastically reduce the value of the U.S. Dollar, and cause a major depression.

2. **'The Blowback Triology'**, three books by Chalmers Johnson (Blowback-2000, Sorrows of Empire-2004, Nemesis-2007). Johnson shows how our meddling, and expensive, foreign policy does more harm than good.

3. **'The Price of Loyalty'**, 2004. by Paul O'Neill, former Sec. of Treasury. This book describes the attitudes of the Bush cabal and how they discussed plans to invade Iraq long before 9/11.

4. **'The Fall of the House of Bush'**, by Craig Unger, 2007 (also 'House of Bush, House of Saud); A journalist, he describes; 1. The true story of how the Bush cabal schemed to control the world for religion and money, and 2. The rise and collusion of the neoconservative and christian-right influences in Republican party politics

5. **'A Nation of Sheep'**, 2007, by Andrew Napolitano, (also 'Constitutional Chaos'), is about how Americans accept abuse by the government without complaint or curiosity, as long as the 'good times roll'.

6. **'Index of Economic Freedom'**, annual since 1994, The Heritage Foundation, charts economic success vs freedom; **www.heritage.org**/research/features/index/

7. **'The Israel Lobby'**, Mar-2006, the LONDON REVIEW OF BOOKS, an essay by John Mearsheimer and Stephen Walt, Professors at the University of Chicago, followed in 2007 by their book **'Israel Lobby and U.S. Foreign Policy'.** An analysis of the scandalous illegal and covert operations of Israel's U.S. lobby 'American-Israel Public Affairs Committee' (AIPAC) and how it impacts votes in Congress and election of Congresspersons.

8. **'The True Believer',** by Eric Hoffer, 1951, a book which shows how people join a group or mass movement (nationalist, social, political, religious, 'Global Warming', etc.) to bring a sense of security, power, righteousness, or income to themselves.

9. **'The Great Reckoning: How the world will change in the depression of the 1990s'**, 1991, by J. Davidson and Lord R. Mogg. They warn of economic collapse of the USA due to overspending and Empire-style foreign policy.

10. Older Books that Gave Warning and Good Advice

a. 'The Law', 1850, by F. Bastiat. With his perspective of the French Revolution, he explains the fallacies of Socialism and how it must degenerate into Communism.

b. 'War is a Racket', 1935, by Smedley Butler, Maj. General, US Marines. He charges that war profiteers are behind our wars and they are all crimes.

c. 'Capitalism: The Unknown Ideal', 1967, by Ayn Rand. Discusses both the productive and moral aspects of Capitalism. Comments by Alan Greenspan (before he joined the Fed banksters in DC)

d. 'Truth and Untruth', 1972, by Rep. Paul N. 'Pete' McCloskey Jr. (R, CA-11, 1967). Pete warned us about Nixon's lies concerning Vietnam, and the broader scope of dishonesty in government. Pete was my Congressman, and I helped in his first election campaign in 1967.

e. 'A Time for Truth', 1979, by William Simon. Bill warned us of the damage being caused by excessive spending, taxes, and the debasement of our currency.

f. 'An American Renaissance', 1979, by Rep. Jack Kemp. Jack sent an upbeat message on how less government spending and lower taxes would produce more growth, all based on his support of Austrian economics. His landmark **'Economic Recovery Tax Act of 1981' (Pub.L.** 97-34), also known as the **ERTA** or "**Kemp-Roth Tax Cut**," was a federal law enacted in 1981.

g. 'Restoring the American Dream', 1979, by Robert Ringer. Robert warned us of a trend in the USA to expect a 'free lunch', and how we can reverse the trend with more personal responsibility and less government.

h. 'A Call for Revolution', 1993, by Martin Gross. This is a list of what's wrong with our economy, culture and government, and how to fix it. It resembles my book 'Rebuild America Now'.

C. Info Sources on Economics and Government:

a). Organizations:
Free-market and limited-government oriented essays, books, blogs, meetings, and courses.

1. **The Cato Institute**: www.cato.org
2. **The Independent Institute**: www.independent.org
3. **The Ludwig von Mises Institute:** Daily essays are at
www.LewRockwell.com, plus books and articles at
mises.org.
4. Reason Foundation: A magazine and **www.reason.org**
5. The Dollar Vigilante: Essays and seminars on how to avoid
losses due to fall of the USA economy and its' money.
www.DollarVigilante.com
6. Foundation for Economic Education: **www.Fee.org**

b). Internet Sites:
1) Web Sites about money and gold: visit
en.wikipedia.org/wiki/Money_supply, fgmr.com,
soundmoneydefense.org, gold.org, Mises.org,
DollarCollapse.com, **goldmoney.com**, **cmre.org**,
en.wikipedia.org/wiki/History_of_money, **goldismoney.info**,
pgpf.org, **measuringworth.com**, **MoneyWatch.com**,
transaction.net/money/lets/, **xat.org/xat/moneyhistory**,
321Gold.com, GATA.org, Kitco.com,

**2). General Web Sites about Government & Economics:
See a flow of essays from; PaulCraigRoberts.org,**
LewRockwell.com, **Activistpost.com**, Antiwar.com, FFF.org,
R. Ebeling- Citadel.edu, **J. Salerno- Pace.edu,
AmericansforProsperity.org**, VDare.com, reason.org,
pacificreasearch.org, **freedomforceinternational.org,**
independent.**org, pacificlegal.org, online.barrons.com,
garynorth.com, dailyreckoning.com**, pgpf.org, **mises.org**,
shadowstats.com, **economicpolicyjournal.com,
zerohedge.com, informationclearinghouse.info,**
The**BurningPlatform.com, trendsresearch.com,
freedomworks.com, campaignforliberty.org,
USDebtClock.org** , the economiccollapseblog.com,
economiccollapsenews.com, (www.dollarvigilante.com,
tdvoffshore.com, **tdvwealthmanagement.com,
tdvpassports.com).**

#2. Glossary:

A. Economics: (Types, or 'Schools of Thought')

1. **'Austrian School'** of economic thought (Hayek, von Mises, Rothbard), emphasizes the spontaneous organizing power of free market pricing, decisions by individuals, gold as money, and little or no government management or stimulation of the economy.

2. Capitalism - An 'economic system' based on private ownership, free enterprise, and minimal regulation. It offers more than economic results. **It is a moral system** that depends on willing buyers and sellers within the rule of law, not coercion and control by others. It has been re-defined as a mean, self-centered, you're on your own, 'social system' by those who prefer Socialism (sharing by force, causing a more equal but lower standard of living for all). The U.S. now has **'Crony Capitalism'**, a damaging distortion where firms get favors from government (often in exchange for campaign donations!). We are further abused by being an **Oligarchy (or Plutocracy)**, where the wealthy 1% have broad control.

3. Communism: The government owns all housing, agriculture, industry and transportation (almost everything but the clothes on your back). The government tells you where to live, go to college (if any), and where to work.

4. Fascism allows private ownership of businesses, but there is extensive government control and preeminence.

5. 'Keynesian Theory' (started by J. M. Keynes in 1933; now used by Krugman, Samuelson, Stiglitz, Bernanke) depends on massive use of government fiscal (spending) and monetary policy (interest rates, money supply), in trying to create prosperity or avoid and end depressions.

History and logic show the Keynes approach is unsustainable and never works for more than a year or two (longer if supported by natural resources; oil, timber, mining, etc.). I say academic folks like it because it provides jobs and grants to them.

6. Monetarism: An approach identified with the 'Chicago School' of economics was led by the late Prof. Milton Friedman Ph.D. of the University of Chicago. It emphasizes management of the money supply by the Fed to control inflation and GDP growth. Most Monetarists dislike the gold standard as 'too inflexible' in changing the money supply. They are wrong because they ignore (or haven't thought of) how the purchasing power of gold per gram increases with more demand. Thus, there is always 'enough'. They claim to like 'free markets', but also like the Fed; a conflict!

7. Socialism: Most of the means of production and trade (factories, railroads, etc) are owned by the government, which sets pricing, product types, etc. The government controls most wages, with an emphasis on 'fairness', need, and 'hours worked', rather than value of the service performed. High, and steeply progressive, taxes support a 'single-payer health system and pension plan

8. 'Supply-Side' : This emphasizes increasing the incentive to invest by reductions in; **a.** capital gains and income taxes (focusing on lower marginal rates), and **b.** regulation. These should be the first steps to revive a troubled economy because they have the lasting effect of stimulating action by producers and investors (on the 'supply', not 'consumer-demand', side) which increases jobs and the GDP. "Supply-Side' was originated by economists P. C. Roberts Ph.D., Robert Mundell Ph.D., and Arthur Laffer Ph.D., and politicians Pres. Ronald Reagan and Rep. Jack Kemp in the 1980s.

B. Commodity: Commodity goods and services are deemed the same (within a type, purity, etc.) without regard to location, market, or who produced it. The price of a commodity good is determined as a function of its market as a whole (all locations, and not a particular dealer). Generally, these are basic resource and agricultural products such as gold, iron ore, sugar, and rice. Soft commodities are goods that are grown, while hard commodities are ones that are extracted through mining.

C. Free Market: A **market** which is free from government intervention (i.e. no regulation except to prevent force, theft and fraud; no subsidies; no monopoly **monetary system**; and no governmental monopolies). In a free market, property rights (ownership of goods and services) are voluntarily exchanged at a price arranged solely by the mutual consent of sellers and buyers, with no government control of pricing, creation of new firms, pay and benefits, hiring and firing, etc. The government's only role is to protect the rights of its citizens and legal visitors.

D. Gang Theft: This occurs when one group of people in some manner over-power another group, and forcibly take assets from them. Most people agree that it is immoral, and should be illegal, but oddly, most people (Liberals and Conservatives) believe it is OK to employ gang-theft-by-vote to tax, restrict, or control others (usually higher tax rates on 'the rich' or 'more privileged'; note that they already pay more per person even with a flat-rate tax!), via government power as the larger group sees fit. **This in fact describes an immoral government.**

E. Greed: An excessive desire for advantage or benefits that ends up hurting the seeker. Examples are: 1. investing in high-risk securities, and losing, 2. breaking laws and policy, and getting caught, or 3. working so hard that you hurt your health and family. This is not to be confused with 'Success', defined below. Liberals and Progressives often view them as the same, based on the false assumption that most 'successful' people are also greedy and have immoral or 'unearned' or 'luck' income. This helps them justify their 'tax the rich' schemes. (see 'Gang Theft' above)

F. Honor: A person gains honor by ethical, meritorious, principled, conduct, which may be performed even when his/her conduct is unknown to others.

G. Loyalty: 1. Faithful to lawful government, 2. True to any person to whom one owes fidelity,

H. Misconduct: 1. Corruption: Illegal acts, **2. Abuse:** Unethical, but not illegal

I. Neo-Conservative: Neoconservatism (commonly shortened to neocon) is a political movement born in the United States during the 1960s among Democrats who became disenchanted with the party's domestic and especially foreign policy. Neoconservatives played a major role in promoting and planning the **2003 invasion of Iraq** (which included defense of Israel).[1] Prominent neoconservatives in the George W. Bush administration included **Paul Wolfowitz**, **John Bolton**, **Elliott Abrams**, **Richard Perle**, J. Gaffney, and **Paul Bremer**. Pres. George W. Bush listened closely to neoconservative advisers regarding foreign policy, especially the defense and growth (land, water, etc.) of Israel. There have been questions of their dual-loyalty (USA vs Israel), and which is first. Publications are Commentary and The Weekly Standard. Read more at; AIPAC.org, https://en.wikipedia.org/wiki/Neoconservatism, **and P.C. Robert's Feb-2016;** http://www.paulcraigroberts.org/pages/books/the-neoconservative-threat-to-world-order/ .

J. Political 'Establishment': The group of people who wield power to change the views and goals of politicians to serve their own interests, using money (campaign donations or secret bribes), political help, or threats of political damage.

K. Principle: An underlying guide to thinking and action.A comprehensive and fundamental law, doctrine, or assumption. A rule, or code of conduct. "Principles are intended especially to guide our behavior in difficult circumstances. If they don't do so, then our proclaimed principles stand revealed as having been nothing but rhetoric in the worst sense of the word.", Robert Higgs, Independent.org. Principles can be refined over time, but not based on needs of the moment.

L. Sacrifice; Voluntary giving of some desirable thing in behalf of a higher, noble, claim

M. Statist: A **political viewpoint** that **sovereignty** is vested not in the **people** but in the national state, and that all individuals and associations exist only to enhance the power, the prestige, and the well-being of the state. The fascist concept of statism repudiates individualism and exalts the nation as an organic body headed by the Supreme Leader and nurtured by unity, force, and discipline (by Wikipedia). An example is Pres. Obama.

N. Success with Honor: The seeker achieves goals in a principled, productive, lawful, sustainable, and ethical way.

#3. Biography of Dave Redick

Personal: Dave grew up with his two brothers in a middle class family near Detroit, MI. When he was 14, the family moved to an 80-acre general farm near Ann Arbor, Michigan. He has an honorable discharge from the U.S. Army Reserve.

Education and Business: Dave won a four-year tuition scholarship to the University of Michigan, based on grades, activities (Sr. Class President, sports), and need, and started in the fall of 1953. He completed his engineering degree in Feb., 1958. Upon graduation he worked as an aerospace engineer for 5 years (rocket engines and satellites) in California, and then started his career in telecom sales and management. In 1965 he earned an MBA in Economics from Santa Clara University in Santa Clara, CA, and
after management positions in several other firms, in 1995 became VP Sales, then President, of a wireless engineering consulting firm **www.hntelecom.com**. He left in 2000 to be VP and cofounder of a Silicon Valley telecom startup 'Fiberstreet' (closed, see Google), and helped raise $6 million of venture capital.
In 2005 he started 'Sustainable Energy Earth', an energy consulting firm.
In 2012 he started Safer Investing Group, which offers information, not advice, to investors (www.SaferInvesting.org).

Political: In 1978, Dave became concerned about economic and social damage caused by counterproductive
government 'management'. He then read about and discussed this subject widely and became an activist for more cost-effective, and less abusive, government. He ran for Congress as a Libertarian in 1982 in District CA-1 (got 3% of vote), then returned to his Republican roots and ran in CA-1 again in 1984 with Reagan (got 38% with same issue positions!). He ran for State Legislature in 2004 as a Republican in District CA-24, and in WI-77 in 2010.
 During the G. W. Bush administration, Dave became concerned about the Republican Party's departure from its core principles. In 2008 Dave founded the 'Forward USA Foundation' to promote better government. The website is www.SAferInvesting.org.

#4. Other Books by Dave:

First edition dates are shown, but all books have been updated as needed. All are 6X9 in. paperbacks and are available at on-line stores such as Amazon.com.

1. 'Monetary Revolution USA', Aug-2017, 148 p.; Presents the history status, problems, and solutions for our monetary system.

2. 'How to Protect and Grow Your Wealth', Aug-2017, 106 p.; Why the value of the U.S. Dollar is declining, and how to choose assets in stronger currencies and safer places.

.

#5. Index

This Index shows key topics from all the Articles in this book. It is a unique collection showing the broad interest in these topics among the Articles. Page numbers in bold show primary info.